Life in a Spacesuit

Anatomy for Mystics

Life in a Spacesuit

Anatomy for Mystics

Michael Rosen-Pyros

Red Fire Publications

Sarasota, FL

ISBN: 978-0-9892616-0-9

Website: www.barefootchiropractor.com
Contact: barefootchiropractor@gmail.com

Cover design: Jade Gates ©
Interior design: Gus Yoo
Editing: Stephanie Gunning

1. Anatomy 2. Yoga 3. Massage 4. Mysticism
5. Biological sciences 6. Personal Health 7. Meditation

Contents

For Andy

We are not our bodies.
Each of us is a soul contained in a spacesuit we call a body.

We study anatomy and physiology becuse spiritual perception is
somatic, and the body is the vehicle for all sensation and perception,
inner and outer.

—Michael Rosen-Pyros

Introduction

Life in a Spacesuit tells the story of life inside and outside the human spacesuit. It is a story that encompasses the life of the Earth and her children, which includes us: the human community. It tells the story of the cells that form the individual body, and the atoms that bond and form the individual cells. It is about the imperatives that derive from the interaction of the multiple dimensions of human experience, realms that are simultaneously operating and overlaid one on top of the other. The story brings together viewpoints that I've drawn from both the sacred and secular traditions of human inquiry.

This book expresses some of the many ideas and images that have been explored in classes, my practice, and my private life. Foremost among these is the idea that the human body is a *spacesuit*, a living laboratory that houses a transient soul. (I also agree with my friend Jeffrey, who refers to life as "voluntary participation in an experimental spiritual rehab program.")

The different varieties of religious experience, to paraphrase William James, are a personal somatic perception. For spiritual perception to happen there must be organic indicators responsive to spiritual phenomena that enable an individual to become aware of, or perceive them. The perception of an inner Self, contained within a body is a spiritual perception, and the ability to reach the conclusion of being a spiritual presence inhabiting a physical form originates within the range of our somatic sensing. In other words, our bodies are vehicles for knowing our seemingly silent, yet ever-whispering Selves.

The story I wish to tell is for those of us who *dream* something about a Self that's part of, yet exists beyond our bodies. We use words like soul, *atman, jiva*, the Force, the astral body, the energy body, and the intuitive self to describe this spiritual presence we are. Words exist in every language and tradition to describe it.

Many people have considered the possibility that there is something we continue to be after our physical lives end. Even better, they perceive that there's a *"me"* that came before their incarnation in their bodies and so they believe this will continue after their bodies have tired of amassing and assembling molecules, both for *them* and for the Earth.

Many of us accept the possibility that our spacesuits provide a *way of knowing* the timeless me that each of us identifies with, and that our Self-knowing is the reason why we're even here—in a body that resides on Earth—in the first place.

Any intuitive dream is housed in the human body, which projects a somatic experience of perceptions, interpretations, and traditions to our mind, wherever that is! This intuitive sense is reinforced by power stories: scriptures, thoughts, and vibrations from great teachers throughout human history. Power stories resonate with truth, joy, and love.

As we look deep inside the spacesuit together, we shall see many worlds, in different magnifications and time frameworks. These worlds, or *realms* of the atom, the cell, the body, and the planet, are comprised of forces that are both opposing and complementary. Positive and negative, full and empty, all are present in their own time and resolved by what I perceive as the subtle and omnipresent *principle of cooperation.* Our lives depend on the precise and constant changes that occur within us between atoms, between cells and between organ systems. Our lives also depend on the precise and constant changes that occur outside us: human beings interacting within their local bioregion, and interacting with each other. As a final "feature" of the spacesuit, there is also the interaction between each of us with the Divine.

The spacesuit is complicated, and the more we perceive the complexity, the more vulnerable we feel. My experience has taught me that it is both difficult and frightening to look this closely at our inner and outer being, the macro-self and the micro-self, and so we avoid the study. But as Mary Rosen-Pyros used to affirm: "Go with fear, my friend!"

To study the human spacesuit is difficult because the body is complicated, and the language of the life sciences is foreign to most of us and seemingly unattainable. Yet any foreign language can be learned. It just takes patience, perseverance, and practice. *Life in a Spacesuit* will present you with terms that may be new to you, or familiar. Though foreign to our modern ears, the language of the life sciences uses ancient words for common things. *Brachium* means "arm" and *cephalic* means "head," words that were commonly spoken in ancient Greece.

I have a suggestion: As you read this book, speak some of

the new, unfamiliar words out loud. Language, in its origin, is spoken and heard. If we say the words we read, and consider their translations, they become more ingrained in our brains, establishing patterns in different regions of the cerebrum, and through that process, more familiar to our ears. Try it and see. (In physiology, "more ingraining" is called *appreciation*. Isn't that sweet?)

It is my favorite hope that this story about living in this spacesuit amuses, informs, and reminds you of our ultimate lightness and interconnectedness. Maybe it will help you to see the tiny, cooperative beings of atoms, molecules, and cells that comprise you and keep you breathing, walking, and doing everything else you say "you" do.

Maybe we'll see, through this investigation, that we are operating on a need-to-know basis with our sensations, emotions, and thoughts, and that the decisions we appear to make are actually the result of the cooperation of trillions of cells.

Maybe we'll be reminded that as a species we aren't necessarily competitive by nature, but, as every hippy (and anthropologist) knows, very cooperative, caring, and loving.

Maybe we will see how big a secret we to ourselves—our conscious and unconscious energies bouncing around and around inside this body of ours, until our final "pink slip" arrives, and we kick ourselves the hell out of there!

Maybe it will make us laugh and feel lighthearted.

Maybe, just maybe, we can be a little more *impressed* with who each of us are. Wouldn't that be something!

Chapter 1

Life in a Spacesuit

"Lost in your eyes
As you hurry by."
—Yes

R emember the movie *Back to the Future?* In an early scene, Dr. Emmett Brown of 1955 observes the 1988 Marty's repeated use of the term "heavy" when meaning "profound." Dr. Brown first says something like: "There's that word again, 'heavy.'" Then he asks, "Is there some problem with the Earth's gravitational pull in 1988?"

Lost in the heaviness of the day, we often forget how *light* we are. Our conversations are replete with a vocabulary that includes words like "work," "pressure," "deadlines," "money," "obligations," and the two certainties of American culture: taxes and death. Who has time to for things other than those required in what we all refer to, as ridiculous as it may be, as the *"real world"*: the one where you get paid, the one where you cover up your body, hide your feelings, and obey idiotic, or even offensive, directives?

Who has time to remember how *light* we are?

All that activity, all that worry, all that pressure, and yes, all that accomplishment and sense of satisfaction in the social and physical world—that is to say, life on Planet Earth—is done in the body, that miracle of miracles that keeps fooling us into looking outside for miracles.

PRESSURE

Let us begin our journey by looking at pressure, one of the physical forces of the Earth. In the science classes and laboratory experiments we did in school, care was taken to note and control the *three basic conditions* of the physical world: pressure, temperature, and volume. Our bodies, these spacesuits living on the Earth, function as living laboratories that constantly monitor these same conditions of pressure, temperature, and volume in the environments that flow both within and outside us.

We know many things about *pressure*, or that which presses. We perceive pressure in our external environment when we enter a pool of water and feel the squeeze around us. The brain senses the pressure change, and signals the cognitive centers so that we notice.

Simple, right?

Not so!

In a short time of continued sensation, the brain concludes that there is no threat from the pressure of water and then decides to *discontinue* its signals to the cognitive centers that perceive pressure. As a result, we *cease* to perceive the squeezing sensation, *even though the sensory neurons continue to monitor the sensation.* This brain-telling-us-what-we-should-perceive is like the classified government information you see in action movies, when spies are informed only on an as-needed basis. It's as though we have low security clearance status in our own living environments.

Pressure as a natural force is so important that we have a specific community of brain cells, an entire pool of *sensory neurons,* devoted only to that force. Cells that register pressure are *mechanoreceptors.*

You can always tell that some force, element, or molecule is important to the body when entire communities of cells are focused upon it. We'll see this principle over and over. It is an important *clue* to understanding the spacesuits we inhabit.

There are five types of sensory neurons. We'll start with mechanoreceptors and meet the rest of them later. Anatomists get pretty specific. But why not? There's so much in there. I mean, in here! Where do I mean?

PRESSURE CELLS: MECHANORECEPTORS

Neurons are an electric tag team. Physiologists would say they carry an electric impulse from one location to another. Neurons are like living extension cords, conveying signals like phone wires. So when we enter a swimming pool, it is the mechanoreceptors of our spacesuit that *feel* (sense) pressure on their small bodies, and they send the message, *"I've been pushed!"* to one part of the brain. The brain then decides whether or not to relay the information to other areas of the brain for us to *feel* (perceive) it. *Sensing* is what the spacesuit does through the neurons. *Perceiving* is what we do!

Having fun yet?

Our spacesuit can sense (and therefore we perceive) pressure from within and from without. It senses the stomach's fullness from within while it feels human touch from without. Both senses are "felt" by the same type of neuron, the mechanoreceptor.

So our bodies live on Earth, and the Earth's atmosphere and water are environmental *pressure systems*, pressing into the body, a spacesuit designed to accommodate that pressure system. At the same time the spacesuit must accommodate the internal pressures from its own biology pressing outward.

INSIDE THE SPACESUIT: SOME BASICS

The body as a self-maintaining spacesuit can be simplified by visualizing cells. When I think of cells, I like to think of them as "really little people." Cell people!

Once upon a time, life organized itself as ocean-born, unicellular organisms. Life remained in this form for billions of years. These organisms were the first cell people. They condensed, differentiated, and complexified themselves until they ultimately formed multicellular organisms. In doing so, life processes realized and manifested the principle of cooperation inherent in the possibilities provided by the ever-changing conditions on Planet Earth.

Cells are the manufacturing centers of the spacesuit. The sum total of their biochemical activity is what we call *metabolism*. Cell people live to manufacture molecules! They make molecules out of other molecules, while generating, condensing, and storing energy.

Although we think of the body—or ourselves—as performing actions like walking or grasping, the actual "doers" are the cell people who reside in and are contained within us. These actions are their synchronized actions. The cell people of the spacesuit, who themselves are made of molecules and energy, are primarily molecule and energy manufacturing centers, performing what I like to imagine as the *dance of the elements.*

In the cellular realm of magnification, the movement of molecules and ions is the story. Life on Earth facilitates the interaction of these atomic beings on three levels: on the Earth's surface, in the environment inside our spacesuit, and finally, within the bodies of the cell people. All these comprise simultaneous *planes of existence.*

Food, air, and water (solids, gases, and liquids) are the three material forms by which the spacesuit can take in the basic ingredients of our inner "soup," our internal environment, requisite for the dance of the elements to take place. This soup feeds the cell people, and they in turn provide a place for molecules and the elements to dance.

I had a physiology teacher who made this statement: "When we look at the sum total of the body's function, the net result is the production and storage of energy!" I never forgot this idea (obviously!) and it has come up again and again as I look at the continuum of matter and energy, and the body's place in the dance of the elements. (Thank you, Dr. Cubina.)

You may remember from elementary school on up how when teachers spoke of the universe, they used the word *"entropy"* to explain the tendency of the universe to unravel, disorganize, and dissipate energy. But as we've already seen, the phenomenon of life on Earth breaks the entropy rule. Rather than dissipating energy, *it concentrates it!* Energy from the Sun is transformed, conformed, transmuted, transmogrified, translated, and transumed into living beings.

Physical life, dancing within an air, water, or earth environment, is an interaction with planetary forces, elements, and molecules. The spacesuit brings these elements into itself through breathing air, eating foods, and drinking liquids, which are mixed within the separated fluids of our digestive organs, absorbed in our bloodstream, distributed to the tissues as extracellular fluid, and are acted upon by the cell people.

A cell, too, is composed of a "body" dancing with and mixing the same forces, elements, and molecules through the separate fluid media found within the cell's body. And when we eat and drink, the digestive organs of the spacesuit break down the solids and liquids, reducing them to tiny chemical building blocks small enough to pass through cell membranes. These molecules are what cell people eat. (Oh, sorry! Cell people don't really eat; they absorb.)

The body is not only a community of cell people; it is also a mirror, a metaphor of the Earth's terrain. The spacesuit is a moving mountain, with an internal ocean and river system, surrounded by a waterproof covering. It maintains itself in balance.

The internal rivers of the spacesuit comprise what anatomists call the cardiovascular, lymphatic, and genitourinary systems. The systematic cooperation of muscle and bone provide the means for this walking stalactite to walk and move rivers of blood around. The waterproof covering, referred to as the skin by most people, and the *integument* by anatomists, is multilayered, as is the atmosphere that covers the Earth.

The respiratory organs move the winds, and absorb the necessary gaseous elements. Lungs actually look like trees turned inside out. They are even referred to as the respiratory or bronchial "trees." The inward movement of oxygen is vital to us, while the outward movement of carbon dioxide is vital to the trees on our planet. (Trees are feeding trees. I love it!)

The idea of the output of trees feeding lungs while lungs feed trees with their output is a reminder that in addition to keeping us alive, our spacesuit also serves as manufacturing centers for the needs of the plant beings that inhabit this planet. The body produces feces (fertilizer), urine (nitrogen-fixing compounds), and carbon dioxide (gas for plant respiration and glucose formation). These molecules are referred to as *metabolic waste products* in the life sciences; but as you can see, there is no waste on Earth. That's only the way we think!

The body is beautiful, so beautiful, in fact, that we can't help ourselves when we see a painting or a statue depicting its form. Our eyes are immediately drawn to its proportion and aesthetics. In spite of our cultural issues with nudity and morality, most of us feel heightened by viewing an artist's rendition of the spacesuit.

It is a blessing and an honor to be housed in this body. May we all work together in the mutual affirmation of the divinity in each of us. May we all nourish this thought, and grow in ways that amplify this vision.

Now on to the spacesuit! Together, let us marvel at our simplicity within complexity. Let us spend some time with each of the parallel and simultaneous realms of our spacesuit: the atomic, cellular, somatic, planetary, and *soular* realms comprised of complementary and opposed forces resolved by the principle of cooperation—which is to say, divine love.

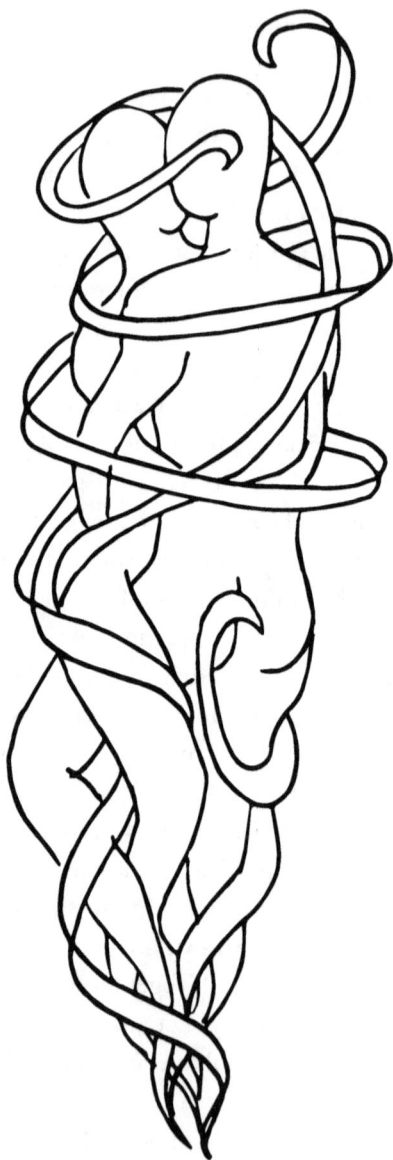

Chapter 2

The Atomic Realm
The Electrical
Sacrifice of Bonding

"The best cooks are the best chemists."
—L. Joseph Roy, RIP

Visualize an atom's body. See a central nucleus of energy, a core made of two subatomic particles: *protons* and *neutrons*. Next, see this central nucleus/core surrounded by a cloud, formed by a third type of particle: *electrons*. Electrons have two motions. An orbit describes the electron's movement around the nucleus, while a *spin* describes the electron's motion in place. The direction (vector) of spin-motion generates another force: *magnetism!* It is magnetism, rather than electrical charges, that impose the attractive forces causing atoms to bond.

Now, refocus your vision. Turn the inner microscope into a telescope. If you expand and expand your inner telescope, you will see our solar system circling a central core, or nucleus, if you will, of energy: the Sun. Like an atom, the Sun is surrounded by planets that orbit and spin like electrons. What we see is continuity at opposite ends of our viewpoint as we shift our level of magnification from the realm of atoms to the realm of cells, then organisms, then planets, and then solar systems. From there, we see solar systems are parts of galaxies.

What about galaxies? Those angelic, spiraling forms are not unlike the double helix formations in the DNA molecule or the kundalini energy in our spine, spiraling upwards and away from the Earth's gravitational forces, which are constantly pulling it down.

THE DANCE OF THE ELEMENTS AND BONDING

The atomic realms are as profound and vast as the realms of outer space. In fact, the distance between the electrons and the nucleus of an atom is relatively the same, in proportion to their microscopic size, as the distance between the planets and the sun in our solar system. It is on the atomic level of magnification that the mysterious exchanges (including mutations) between matter and energy take place. All this is going on outside and inside of this body, this spacesuit.

The atomic realm is driven by the physical and life forces of the Planet Earth. In the spacesuit where we live, atoms and molecules are contained in an ecosystem that keeps them under the constant, appropriate "laboratory" conditions of temperature, pressure, and volume. Their quantities are kept in balance by many systems of the body, including most especially the nervous and endocrine systems, which are responsible for monitoring and modifying the internal environment of our spacesuit. The atomic realm is a mosaic of infinite wonder.

In light of all this, I wonder, how many of us know and love chemistry? *Hmm.* Let's have a show of hands. Anybody? *Hmmm.*

Just as I thought!

Yet we lie when we say we don't know or like chemistry, because we confront atomic realities throughout our daily lives. We actually practice a lot of chemistry; we just don't call it that. For instance, when we desire sugar, and eat a doughnut instead of Belladonna (which is poisonous), we are in fact exercising a long tradition of chemistry. We all know about the importance of oxygen for breathing, even if we don't know details; and we know something about carbon monoxide poisoning, though we may not be sure what the poison does.

We know about stomachs that had too much pepperoni-with-red-pepper-added pizza or beer, or, hopefully, both. And we have on occasion been known to take an *antacid* after eating said pizza, although the topic of alkalinity, acidity, and pH may shut down our brains and turn on our sleep mode in chemistry class. We know something about eating and the four groups of food, though we may not think in terms of carbohydrate, protein, lipid, or nucleic acids.

We have heard of unsaturated fat in our cooking oils and peanut butter, though we may not know about long-chain fatty acids. We can see that at room temperature, vegetable oil flows, but lamb fat stays on the muscles of a leg bone (until it is dripped off by prolonged, garlic-stuffed baking). We rarely consider that observation as expressing *properties of lipids* and their physical state at room temperature, yet we see, and therefore know, that animal lipids are relatively solid at room temperature, while those of plants are liquid.

That's why Socrates said that learning is a discovery, or uncovering, of what we already know. (For more on his view on learning, see Plato's dialogue *Meno*.)

The dynamic of atoms seeking magnetic balance generate atomic imperatives that drive our bodies as much as they drive the changes that occur on the surface of the Earth. These imperatives result in somatic actions. As we've already seen in the case of the pressure-sensing mechanoreceptors, the imperatives of the atomic realm are so important to the working of the spacesuit that there are entire populations of cell people that monitor and alter the quantities of many important elements and molecules: hydrogen, oxygen, and carbon dioxide gases, sodium and chloride (salt), potassium, calcium, water, and other members of the atomic realm.

BACK TO BASICS: ATOMS, ELEMENTS, AND MOLECULES

As we look at the details of the human body, we see that it is a community of living units called cells, working cooperatively to form this spacesuit. By "working," I mean that the cells are transporting, storing, building, and breaking down the entities of the atomic realm. That's their job. That's what they do. Cell people are micro-manufacturing centers, internally organized much like a factory, on a conveyor belt system, assembling or disassembling molecules that are made from other atoms and molecules.

We know a lot about choosing molecules that are good or bad for us (though we usually refer to the behavior of choosing as responding to hunger). We choose something specific to eat because we find ourselves being "in the mood" for a donut, a bagel, or a blintz! Or we want a hamburger or rice and beans. We don't usually think of choosing a food as the selection of a particular molecule, like a carbohydrate or protein. But that's what it boils down to. Because that's how the cell people think! (Or how I imagine cell people think.)

I wasn't always this way, you know! I used to hate this stuff—especially the chemistry. But then I had a great chemistry teacher in Locust Valley High School, L. Joseph Roy. Mr. Roy started out the course by explaining that chemistry is about cooking, and that "the best cooks are the best chemists." Since I grew up with Greeks, who are some of the best cooks I know, I understood his meaning. (And yes, I was one of those fat Greek kids!)

Mr. Roy's love for the elements was contagious. Though I failed out of his course the first quarter, I took it the next year and excelled beyond my expectations. Such was the degree of his inspiration. The rest was, well, a lot of reading, memorizing, and reflecting. His secret: He loved kids! Look back at every teacher you thought great, and you'll see that, for the most part, they were advocates, not adversaries. So let me take a moment and offer thanks to all the champions of students' minds. (Amen!)

In Mr. Roy's memory, let's talk a little more about chemistry and cooking. While making chicken soup, we can "tell" if it "needs" salt. We think and say the *chicken soup* needs the salt, when, in fact, it is we who require the intake of salt. Then again, it's not really *us*, but the cell people that require the salt. They let us know, then, as we taste, whether we "think" that the soup contains enough, too much, or too little salt,

Salt is so important to the spacesuit that there exists a population of cells whose job it is just to taste for salt. We learn to attach the words "too little," "too much," and "enough" (or as Goldilocks put it, "Just right!") to the *perceptual judgment* of *balanced saltiness*, but the perception is based on the needs of the cell community, and, of course, us, at the same time.

METABOLISM

I like to make the science of chemistry fun by thinking about it as sex. Truly! I think of it as a social relation between "atomic people." (Surprised? Why? After all, if cells can be people, then why not atoms?) The forces of attraction and repulsion between atoms result in either the forming or the breaking up of *bonds*, or "Who's doing who?" and "Who broke up?" Chemistry describes the *bonds* that take place between atoms, and the products that these combinations form: *molecules* and *ions*. Chemical bonds are the prototype of the bonds that take place between each of us: a mirror of the bonds taking place within, outside, and between us. Chemical bonds are the result of magnetic forces between atoms and molecules.

Let's return to the dance of the elements. The dynamics of the atomic realm, which occur within the living spacesuit, manifest as a great *dance* in and around cellular populations. The cell people are the centers of controlled chemical reactions. What's going on?

There are only two possible dance steps. In the first, the atoms respond to the forces of attraction by building molecules out of raw materials received from the waters that surround the cell people. The building of chemical entities by bonding is called *"anabolism."* The second dance step is about the opposite process, the *breaking down* of chemical bonds: *catabolism*.

Now take a global view of the sum total of all chemical reactions, all the building and breakdown of molecules in our bodies. That's *metabolism.*

That's it, folks! That's chemistry. The atomic realm alive within us involves the building and breaking of bonds. The rest is gossip about details: Which atoms find each other attractive, come close to each other, and exchange energies? Which molecules are broken up, and what internal or external energies were causative? By this process molecules are born. It's that simple!

ATOMS ARE (ELECTRIC) PEOPLE, TOO!

Atoms are like mini-solar systems. They have a central core of energy particles, the *nucleus,* and an outer ring of orbiting particles, the *electrons.* As complicated as the spacesuit may be, it is nevertheless the product of these tiny "building blocks" of light in motion: the *elements.* There are ninety-two naturally occurring atomic elements found on Earth. Most interesting is that out of those ninety-two elements, most of the body (96 percent) is comprised of only four: carbon, oxygen, hydrogen, and nitrogen. You've more than likely heard of these four elements.

Now I need to get a little technical (okay, A LOT technical) in order to describe the body parts of the atomic people. Now get small again. The core structure of the atom, the nucleus, contains two types of particles: *protons* and *neutrons.* Protons carry a positive electric charge,while neutrons carry no charge.Electrons, which orbit around the the nucleus, carry a complementary negative electric charge.

The number of protons in a given element is constant. Therefore, an atom is given—nay, designated—an atomic number by the *quantity of protons* in its nucleus. An atom has as many electrons (charge −) as it does protons (charge +). So, for example, hydrogen has one proton and so has the atomic number of 1 and has one orbiting electron. Oxygen, with eight protons and electrons, is designated the atomic number 8. You can see the pattern easily enough, right?

While the number of protons and electrons are always equal for a given element, the number of neutrons may vary. This variation is called an *isotope.*

ISOTOPE FLASHBACK

Do you remember the first time you heard the word *"isotope"*? I do! It was in the 1953 monster movie *The Beast from 20,000 Fathoms.* The only way scientists could figure out how to kill the radioactively resurrected dinosaur that was now menacing the world was to shoot it up with a radioactive isotope! How horrid (and typical)! From then on, the word "isotope" stayed with me. So, there I was, already learning something about chemistry, and I didn't know it.

ATOMIC NUMBER AND ENERGY SHELLS

Electrons traveling in planetary-like orbits around a nucleus move within energy fields called *"electron shells."* These shells can be represented as a series of concentric circles of energy, like layers of clouds, surrounding the nucleus of the atom. Sometimes they are also referred to as *"electron clouds."* (There is subtle poetry in the physical sciences.) Now the layering of shells is important, because attraction and bonding happen *only in the outermost shell.*

We can see this metaphorically with each other. When humans bond physically, in the somatic realm, we don't do it through, say, our livers, which are found deep within the spacesuit. We bond from our outermost layers: the skin, nose, mouth, and ears. The same is true in the cellular realm, where multicellular bonding takes place in the atom's outermost layer: the plasma membrane. Life is consistent in every realm!

Electron shells grow in number as the number of protons (and therefore their atomic numbers) get larger. More and more protons increase the density of the nucleus, and the resultant shells expand with them. The really interesting thing is that except for the first two elements, the *outermost electron shells can only, at maximum, contain eight electrons!* After that, another shell is always generated. I'll tell you why that interests me.

Wait. I'd rather show you.

MUSICAL INTERLUDE

This writer-within-a-spacesuit-musician-wannabe can't help noticing that eight is the number of electrons needed to complete the outer shell of an atom.

Again, what is the magic number for completion?

Eight!

Now consider music. How many notes complete a scale? *Uh huh!* Eight again.

No coincidence! The mystics say the whole universe is a manifestation of consciousness, sound, and light. We are consistent in every realm.

THE ELECTRICAL SACRIFICE OF BONDING

Atoms with less than eight electrons in their outer electron/ energy shells manifest the "desire" or "preference" to complete their outer shells. This desire is resolved through the electrical sacrifice of *bonding.* They seek to have an outer shell of eight, just as in the completion of a musical scale. Atoms join together to reach a common goal—the balance of their magnetic fields—*fulfillment of their outer shells.* (Full-fill.) In so doing, they have formed chemical bonds and created a molecule. This is why the atomic realm is dynamic and volatile.

I should mention that atoms do exist with completed outer rings which, as expected, have little if any interactions. These are called *inert gases.* Helium is an example of an inert gas.

For magnetic balance to occur, atoms either take on or give up one or more electrons. This, however, gives each participating atom a state of what is now *electric imbalance,* while the outer rings are fulfilled and in a state of magnetic balance. These two forces, electric and magnetic, drive the entire atomic realm. Atoms, although *electrically* balanced, are also *magnetically* imbalanced, and so are drawn to other atoms by an innate need for magnetic balance.

There are two forms of chemical bonding. In one type, electrons are transferred from one atom's outer shell to the outer shell of another. Sodium chloride (table salt) is an example of this. This type of bonding is called *ionic* because in water the sodium and chloride, now electrically are torn apart—dissolved—and "wander" in an electrified solution of water, each particle being now being called an *"ion."*

Some day take a look at story of Io in Robert Graves' *Greek Myths.* Jealous of Io, the goddess Hera turned her into a cow, and then sent a gadfly to torment her. Poor woman! Io subsequently wandered all around Europe as a cow, hence the name for ionic bonding.

The second type of bonding is called *"covalent."* Electrons orbit around its own outer shell for a while, then around the outer shell of a second, and then back; while the second atom does the same, both *sharing* their outer-shell energy with each other. Hydrogen and oxygen gases are examples of this type of *covalent* bonding. So is water. The result of both types of bonding—ionic and covalent—is an atomic entity with qualities different and distinct from the atom's original components.

We already know something about magnetic force as it pertains to our spacesuit. We know about it because when two people get together erotically, we say they have a strong "chemistry" between them, or when a speaker is charismatic, we say he or she possesses a "magnetic" quality. On the other hand, if we don't like a person, we might say we are "repulsed" or that the person has bad "vibes." Qualities of attraction and repulsion are exactly what atoms are working with.

Ionic bonds tend to be stronger than covalent bonds because the polarities between the elements in ionic bonds are stronger. As electrons have been either given up or taken on, they no longer orbit their home atom.

Covalent bonds are less strong, and they interact with other covalently bonded molecules more readily. The electrons are shared, so the electron never quite leaves "home" (like it's going to college and still doing laundry at Mom's house).

WATER, pH, AND POLARITY

I want to finish this section by spending a little time with the mother of us all: water. Another of the infinite miracles of Earth's bounty, water deserves attention. It is a molecule made of two species of atom: oxygen and hydrogen. In a water molecule, there are two hydrogen atoms for each oxygen atom. Its chemical formula is something many of us know it by: H_2O. This molecule can be illustrated in the shape of an upside down Y. (Of course, the Y could be right side up, sideways, or coming straight at you, too!)

The bonds in a water molecule are covalent bonds. That means each of the two hydrogen atoms in a molecule shares an electron with the single oxygen atom, spending enough time with the oxygen to satisfy oxygen's desire for the magnetic completion of its shell. At the same time, two of the oxygen atom's electrons are orbiting each of the hydrogen atoms, which is enough to satisfy their two-electron requirement. Everybody's happy!

In water molecules, the electrons spend more time around the oxygen atom than they do around the hydrogen atoms. This makes the oxygen side of the water molecule more negative, while the hydrogen side is subsequently more positive. When a whole molecule has *electricalness* to it, with positive and negative sides, it is called a *polar* molecule.

Sound boring? *Nay!* Read on.

The polarity in water makes it magical. It allows water to perform the miracle of *dissolution*, or dissolving things. Take table salt, which chemistry books always use as an example because it is our most important salt as well as the easiest to explain. Like water, table salt is composed of two types of atoms: in this case, sodium and chlorine. Sodium and chlorine have one and seven electrons in their outer shells, respectively, and their bond is ionic.

Table salt was seen as such an important gift of nature that its Latin name is *naturium*. Isn't that sweet? (Or salty!) Now, put some salt in water and, *voila*, it disappears. Magic!

The polar nature of the water molecule is strong enough to *pull apart* the salt molecule, so that the original atoms that made up the salt aren't bonded anymore. After dissolving in water, these atoms are referred to as sodium and chloride ions, and the water is described as "salty."

Remember, we can know the salt molecule is important to the spacesuit because the spacesuit houses entire populations of cells in our tongues, kidneys, and brains that monitor and adjust the quantities of sodium or chloride present in our bodies.

ACIDS AND BASES (ALKALI)

Acid and *alkaline (base)* are terms that define the "electricness" of any given pool of water. You may be familiar with water that is electrically neutral, or distilled, so necessary when replacing battery fluids in your car. I don't know about you, but after enough scary movies, I was respectfully frightened of working with acids in chemistry labs. Images of flesh peeling off faces, arms, and other body parts provided raw material for nightmares. *Argh!* One that especially comes to mind is *House on Haunted Hill* with Vincent Price. In this 1959 film, his murderous, pretty wife-in-a-slinky-satiny-nightgown gets pushed into a vat of acid by a marionette skeleton. True camp!

So, as scary as acids may be—and bases can be pretty awful, too, as eating soap will attest—let's consider a final, magical piece about the water molecule, what is called *"pH."* Under the right circumstances, the polarity of water is so powerful that water itself can dissolve a few of its floating partners. When it does, it turns into a hydrogen ion (H+) and a hydroxyl ion (OH–).

When there is an overbalance of hydrogen ions, we say the *potential for* hydrogen ion (pH) is greater, and describe that fluid as an *acid*. When there is an overbalance of hydroxyl ions, we say the *potential for* hydrogen ion (pH) is low, and assign a different pH, and describe that fluid as *alkaline*, or sometimes, a *base*.

Acid substances taste "sour." Alkaline substances taste "bitter."

The importance of pH can't be stressed enough, because the human body contains different fluids in separate compartments, and each fluid works only within a certain range of acid or alkaline pH. Anything outside that range renders the cells inefficient, inactive, or even dead. As was true for salt in an earlier paragraph, pH is so important that the spacesuit houses entire populations of cells from the tongue to the kidneys that monitor, in this case, the amount of hydrogen and hydroxyl ions floating around in the bloodstream.

Okay. We're about ready to meet the "people" who live in the cellular realm and work in the *molecular-industrial complex* of the spacesuit. Before we do, please do a simple exercise.

EXERCISE

Sit by a plant and gaze at its leaves while you breathe in and out, a most vital and complementary cycle which physiologists call pulmonary ventilation. Here, in the leaves, while you exhale, plants receive nourishing carbon dioxide, which is the result of your cellular respiration.

Let your breathing deepen. Imagine the air moving into you as streaming from the exhalation of the plant. As you breathe out, imagine the air from your lungs moving into the plant's receiving organs. Back and forth, in and out . . .

See if after a few minutes of this practice, the exchange between you and the plant becomes more than imagined sense.

"WE RECEIVE IN
ORDER TO SHARE."
—QABALIST SAYING

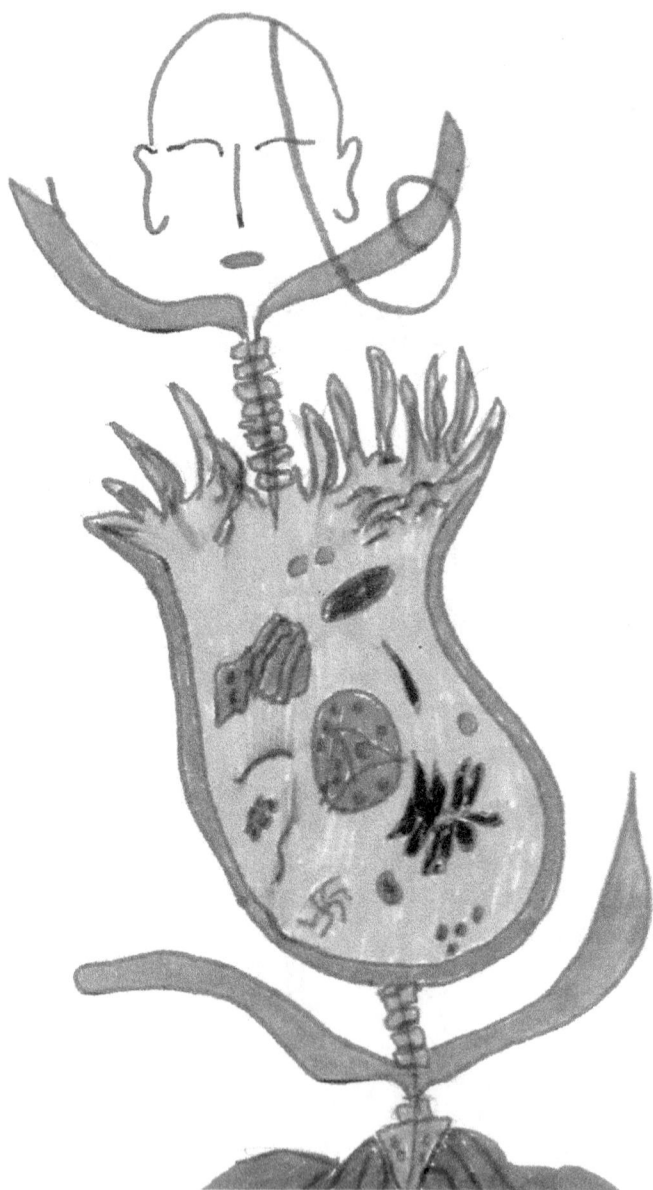

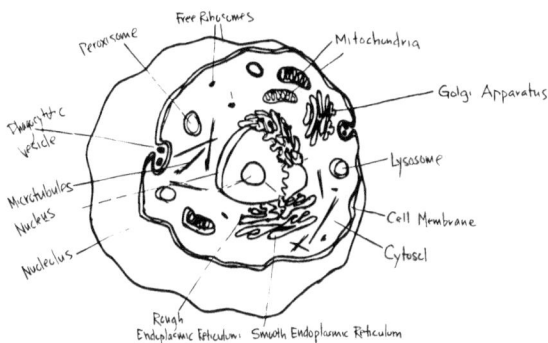

Labels on the diagram: Free Ribosomes, Peroxisome, Mitochondria, Golgi Apparatus, Phagocytic Vesicle, Lysosome, Microtubules, Nucleus, Cell Membrane, Nucleolus, Cytosol, Rough Endoplasmic Reticulum, Smooth Endoplasmic Reticulum

Chapter 3

The Cellular Realm

*"I have been trying to think of the earth as a kind of organism,
but it is no go. I cannot think of it this way. It is too big, too complex,
with too many working parts lacking visible connections. The other night,
driving through a hilly, wooded part of southern New England,
I wondered about this. If not like an organism, what is it like, what is it
most like? Then, satisfactorily for that moment, it came to me:
it is most like a single cell."*
—Lewis Thomas, *Lives of a Cell*

A SPACESUIT COMPRESSED

Consider a single-celled organism, like the amoeba in the illustration above. You may remember looking at amoebae in school while playing with a microscope. I've already told you that, for me, single-celled organisms are more interesting if we consider them little people: cell people. It's fun to think of them as people, because they do what we, living in the spacesuit, do. Single cell people breathe, eat, poop- and- pee, reproduce, move, sit still, and pulsate. They can do this because they have organs similar to ours: *organelles*, meaning "little organs." Organelles are the prototypes for our organs— again with the mirroring!

Actually, it's the other way around! Whatever it is we say we "do" is only possible because of life in the cellular realm and the cell people doing what they do.

THE UNITY OF THE CELLULAR AND
THE SOMATIC REALMS

We hear it all the time. We say it to each other: "It affected me on a cellular level." (What does that mean anyhow? When does anything *not* affect us on a cellular level?) What is a *cell* and what does it have to do with the human spacesuit?

I like to begin by imagining cells as people, *beings* that live in the cellular realm: round, tiny, funny-looking people that resemble jelly candies, with real lives, identities, jobs, relationships, and deaths. If we look at the cell people under a low-powered microscope, we can see they exist in clusters that resemble cities and landforms as viewed from an airplane.

The cellular realm can be compared to a community of individuals, a nation of cell people, trillions of them, in fact, with specific jobs to do. They live in a controlled ecosystem inside the spacesuit—our internal environment—a pool of nutrients surrounded by a waterproof covering we call the skin. Some of these cell people are loners, traveling around by themselves. But most live in clusters of similar cells that do similar jobs as them. These clusters are called *tissues.*

Now think about yourself for a second. In your totality as

a human being, you have a lot in common with cell people. You perceive yourself as an individual—a single entity, a unified whole—with a real life and identity, with love, work, relationships, and the anticipation of death. Yet you are, in fact, a composite of trillions of little cell people who feel the same way! The two realms of existence—yours and your cells—are interlinked, interdependent, and simultaneously occurring.

Like a cell person, you live as part of a community of individuals living in spacesuits, billions of them, in fact; human beings with specific jobs, living in an *ecosystem*, a pool of nutrients, surrounded by an invisible, air-filled "skin" called the *"biosphere."* This level of you is what I refer to as the *somatic* realm, which life scientists refer to as the level of the *organism.*

Cell people live in a shallow, fibrous ocean of fluids and nutrients: their extra cellular fluids (ECF). This same ECF within the spacesuit is an ecosystem, a pool of liquids, ions, and molecules from the atomic realm. (Remember: it is called the ECF from the cell person's perspective; in terms of you in the somatic realm, the same fluid is referred to as the spacesuit's *internal environment*) The internal ecosystem requires replenishment and detoxification on a regular basis. This generates *cellular imperatives* that direct the spacesuit—that is to say *you*—to perform certain activities, such as eating, drinking, warming yourself, or hugging a friend. The spacesuit is self-maintaining through the actions of the cell people, and we call this self-maintenance *"homeostasis."*

Cellular populations operate a replenishment system run by the most extraordinary pair of cells: the neurons and the endocrine cells. These cell people interpret for us what comes in and goes out—in other words, they tell us what travels to and from the external environment (*outside* our bodies) and internal environment (*inside* our bodies/the cell people's external environment). The combined neuroendocrine cells monitor and adjust the spacesuit's "soup ingredients" and inner laboratory conditions of temperature, pressure, and volume.

Let us stop here for a second to "dust off" our inner microscope and review the three environments of the spacesuit. For us in the somatic realm, the *external environment* is the Earth and all her gifts. Our bodily fluids and cell people make up the *internal environment*. However, for the cell people, what we call our internal environment is their external environment (ECF). The internal environment of the cell people is called *"cytoplasm."* The fluid therein is referred to as *"intra cellular fluids"* (ICF). The constituents of cytoplasm represent the cell's inner ecosystem.

The cell, too, is a spacesuit!

Just as the human spacesuit needs to replenish its inner ecosystem, so does the cellular spacesuit of the cell people. Both run the operations of the human spacesuit's organ systems on the macroscopic level, and the cell's organ systems on the microscopic level, resulting in importing, manufacturing, and exporting items to and from the atomic realm.

Going crazy yet? So many of our actions are imperatives devised by the cells in our bodies. We think we're hungry (and we are), yet, at the same time, it is actually our cells sensing the need for the replenishment of molecules and ions to consume and process that makes us feel this way. Sounds like a complex, multidimensional world economy to me! Or like a three-dimensional chess game. As Mr. Spock from *Star Trek* would say, "Fascinating!"

SOME PHILOSOPHY AND METAPHOR

The cell represents one of infinite possibilities of the atomic realm interacting with itself on Earth, manifesting the principle of cooperation in the universe.

Hundreds of millions of years ago, a portion of the beings who lived on the unicellular Earth formed multicellular beings, combining and forming cellular cooperatives, as opposed to going it alone as a unicellular microbe. Our species is often described as social, and, if this is true, it is only true because division of labor and specialization is within the realm of possibilities of the life form called the cell in the first place. This spacesuit, and what it can do, is a magnification of what beings in the cellular realm are capable of doing.

For example, we've seen how if the body breathes, if we breathe, it's because cell people breathe, or have a need to *respire:* They need to take in oxygen and expel carbon dioxide, a process necessary for cellular *and* somatic life.

Breathing has an added complexity on this great laboratory of Earth where we live in our spacesuits. The spacesuit is interactive with, and accommodates the needs of the life forms that also live here, especially the plants. The problem that plants have is that in order to perform *photosynthesis*, or turning sunlight into energy, they require carbon dioxide. This is where we and the other aerobic breathers on our planet come in. We breathe out carbon dioxide that's good for the plants, even as we rid ourselves of a toxic surplus. By breathing out, we *expire* a metabolic waste product that plants need: carbon dioxide.

Now consider this idea: There is no "waste" on Earth. Our waste product is the starting point of the plant respiration cycle: They breathe in carbon dioxide, mix it with sunlight, and make carbohydrates. Plants expel—or breathe out—*their* metabolic *waste product,* oxygen, in the manufacture of carbohydrate. We inspire the oxygen they expel, because we need it for our energy cycles; and we eat them to get the carbohydrates we need.

Hence, plants and humans have a perfect relationship.

I've always admired the plants. First, they were here before we were, and they'll most likely be here when we've gone the way of T-Rex. But what fascinates me is photosynthesis. Plants can absorb sunlight and turn it into carbohydrates and oxygen when it's mixed with chlorophyll and carbon dioxide. The best we can do is to absorb sunlight and watch ourselves get suntans.

Digestion presents a similar tri-level complexity. We say we eat because we're hungry, and so we initiate actions in order to satisfy both our spacesuit and the cell people. But again, there is a third complementary function: the plants need our feces and urine. We defecate the fertilizers and urinate the fixable nitrogen from which plant roots make protein.

In this way the cycle of eating and feeding plants goes on in perpetuity.

Our presence is good for more than just the plants. When we *expire* for the last time, the spacesuits we've inhabited throughout our lives provide a feast for flies, bugs, bacteria, and hordes of creepy-crawlies. People are good for plants, bugs, and bacteria.

If we breathe, eat, digest, absorb, and die, it is because cells absorb and metabolize what we breathe and eat. Cells need food, so we eat plants. The plants also need food, so we pee, poop, and breathe out. We do these things for our cells, for the spacesuit, and for the Earth at the same time.

You live for yourself and the Earth, while the cells live for both their own lives and for the needs of your spacesuit—that is to say, you. It is truly a perfect relationship.

THE ORGANIZATION OF CELLULAR LIFE: CELLS ARE PEOPLE, TOO!

In 1966, the movie *Fantastic Voyage* came to the theaters and took us inside the body in ways never before seen. The vastness of our inner space became a visual experience. And it didn't hurt that the cast looked so good wearing latex! At that point, I was hooked. It was the first time I had gotten a glimpse through an inner microscope. I discovered there was so much to learn about this spacesuit and ourselves by taking a look at the lives of cell people.

Cell people are like us in so many ways, but especially in the way they are cooperative social beings. Our bodies provide an environment for the cell people to live in clusters, populations of similar cells living in similar environments. These clusters can be found as one slices delicately through the layers *(tissues)* of the body. Since the Greek word for "layer" is *"histo,"* the study of cellular layers is called *"histology."*

The beings of the cellular realm within us are not independent like amoebae. They are specialized and rely on the entire bodily system running cooperatively. I know we like to think of our species as competitive, but that's a lot of bunk! I stand by the evidence that says we are cooperative by nature, if the cell people and everything else in the universe are to be believed.

The tissues each have a specific job (what physiologists would call a *"function"*). Yet, each cell person has a twofold purpose: *to maintain itself* (keep alive and be repaired) and *to perform an activity necessary for the spacesuit's function* (for example, to manufacture thyroid hormone or a muscle fiber that contracts on demand). Cell people, the majority of them, live in layers of tissues that are usually separated and/or tied together by glue-like threads called *"collagen."*

Some cell people snuggle together within a sponge-like framework, like the frameworks we see in the liver, kidney, lung, and spleen. Others groups cluster within a muscular framework, like the bladder, stomach, and heart. Still others are contained within a bone or cartilage meshwork. However they group, whenever we see a group of similar cell people with similar jobs, histologists call that cell population a tissue. Tissue groups are known as *"organs."*

THE FOUR TISSUES: HOW THEY LOOK

The microscope has made possible the viewing of complex layers of the spacesuit. In this universe of metaphor, it is not surprising to notice that stained tissues appear like the layers we see in stratified rock that has been cut or eroded. The techniques for surveying human tissues have been refined over the years, and so has our information about them; yet the early workers in the field of histology found that the variety of populations appeared in only four architectural arrangements, and the *four-tissue* tradition of histological description continues today.

Some cell people live side by side with tight junctions, forming single or multiple sheets of cell people. In the life sciences, tightly joined sheets are known as *"epithelia."* These sheets cover and line everything inside the spacesuit, and the cell junctions are so tight that the blood vessels that feed them can't push through, and so live just underneath the sheet.

The second group of cell people live right next to the

epithelia. This second group is not tightly connected; its members often live physically distant from each other. They live in a physical environment that ranges from the bloody, jelly-like, gross stuff we can see in deep cuts of skin, to the solid, rock-like structures of bone. The cell people who live in this particular environment are also responsible for making their environment! This second class of tissue is known as *connective tissue.*

The names of the two remaining tissue groups are familiar to us as *muscle tissue* and *nerve tissue.* These two were grouped not because of how they looked so much as by what they do. Muscle is special in its ability to shorten on demand—the phenomenon of *contraction.* The ability to shorten is a specialty, an elaboration of what all cell people do, which is to *pulsate.*

Pulsation occurs because a cell's inner framework contains a protein that spans its cytoplasm, stretching from inner wall to inner wall, like a papier-mâché frame. The proteins have an electric charge that moves along the protein's surface. As the charge moves, it *folds* the protein portion on which it lies, and *then unfolds* it as the charge continues to move along the molecule. The summation of all this folding and unfolding action appears as pulsation in a unicellular being.

Muscle tissue takes that innate ability of all cell people to pulsate and fills itself (its *cellf?*) with the protein, which, along with signals from the nerve cells, can contract on demand.

Very cool!

Nerve cells, the fourth class of tissue, are real freaks. These cells are called *neurons* and they have two special gifts. First, they can move an electrical current around their bodies in a specific direction, and, second, they can take parts of their "skin," or the *cell membrane*, and stretch it out. (There is a TV cartoon character, Inspector Gadget who stretches his arms and legs as far a he needs to, just like a neuron. Ask your kids about him.)

This membrane—the cell's skin—gets longer and grows with, let's say for an example, the thumb, which starts as a small "limb bud" adjacent to the neuron. By the time the thumb is completed, the neuron responsible for the thumb's sense of touch is already in place on the thumb's surface. Touch sensations in the thumb travel along the neuron's extension up the arm to the nerve cell's body, which actually lives deep in the spinal cord and even, sometimes, as far up as the brain. These long extensions of a neuron are called *axons.*

As we've already seen, each cell person houses an inner ecosystem filled with ions, molecules, and organelles. Most of these molecules possess an electrical charge. If you add up the positive and negative charges of the various entities of the intracellular fluid, you get a resultant *negative charge* inside the cell. Due to this, all cells function as electromagnetic units. What makes neuron tissue so special is its ability to convey electric signals - an energetic expression of consciousness - from one area of the body to another.

The ECF, the fluid outside the cell people, also has a charge—however in this case, a positive charge—which can be measured. (It turns out that in the last century some folks invented a machine, a *microvoltmeter,* that can penetrate both sides of the cell's membrane and quantify the charge running across the membrane.) This charge needs to be maintained by the cell in order to stay alive, and it does so by allowing ions to enter and then pumping them out all day long. All cells do this in order to maintain a steady electrical state. (Remember again that what we are referring to as the ECF - from the perspective of the cell person - is at the same time the ecosystem of the human spacesuit's internal environment, from the perspective of you.)

Nerve tissue cell people take their innate electricalness and "play" with ions in order to *change* their voltage. By doing this, they can move electric current along their Inspector Gadget-like arms as far as they are stretched.

Again, very cool!

ORGANS AND ORGANELLES

The time of gestation in the womb is when the tissues of the spacesuit form into different *organs* (heart, lungs, liver, kidneys, and so on.) They are located in specific areas in order to participate in their given "specialty" within a collective activity, which the life sciences refer to as a *system.*

Consider again the way the organelles of a single cell work to keep that cell alive: Cell people eat, breathe, move ions and molecules in, out, and around; they alter and manufacture new ions and molecules, and move around inside the human spacesuit. Cell people can do so because each has its own spacesuit, and its own *organelles.*

Populations in the cellular realm live in groups, bundles, swellings, and sheets that mirror and amplify the inner ecosystem of *their* own spacesuits. The organs and systems of *our* spacesuits are analogous to those organelles, but on a magnified scale. Organs and organelles mirror each other so well that they often resemble each other.

We've seen this already in plasma membrane resembling the fat layers of our skin. Now I'll offer you some other analogous examples.

AEROBIC CELLULAR RESPIRATION

Cell people breathe. Aerobic breathing is made possible by the presence of organelles called *mitochondria*. It is common knowledge that you and I breathe oxygen-rich air. Then what? The oxygen enters the breathing tube in our bodies called the bronchial tree (which looks, not surprisingly, like a tree inside out), whose branches end in little berry-like layers called *alveolar sacs*. Here, the endpoint of the breathing tube is a single sheet of cell people thin enough for the oxygen to pass through. Which it does. From here oxygen enters the capillaries carrying blood towards the heart, and then it is distributed in the bloodstream to all of the cell people in the body. The oxygen goes into the cell's "lungs," which are the mitochondria.

If you look mitochondria up on the Web, you might be surprised to see that this organelle actually looks like half a lung, though by now we shouldn't be too surprised that organs and organelles are structural and functional metaphors of each other. It is here in the mitochondria that the oxygen "burns" a carbohydrate, and makes energy molecules called adenosine triphosphate (ATP).

Heat, water, and carbon dioxide are the byproducts of this process. Generating energy is a *huge* problem for cells, and for the human spacesuit. For this reason the manufacture of ATP (energy) is one of our primary metabolic activities.

ENZYMES AND METABOLISM

I haven't mentioned enzymes yet, but they are another of the miracle molecules in the human body. They are what I like to think of as the molecular "workers" of the cell. What do I mean by that? Well, let's start by reviewing the idea of metabolism: that the cellular realm is a meeting place for the elements to dance. Recall that what's involved in this dance is the splicing together and the splitting apart of molecules. This work is being done on specific molecules for specific reasons, and the enzymes are the protein molecules that allow this to happen.

All molecules that undergo metabolic change exist as a unique shape with a unique energy configuration. Enzymes are formed so that only one molecule can fit into its "hands." When the molecule is present, the enzyme does its job: It splices or dices.

Enzymes are huge molecules made up of simple protein building blocks called *amino acids*. Enzymes are placed in a row so that after one enzyme does its metabolic job, the next enzyme fits the byproduct, which then which fits onto the next enzyme, and the next until the process is completed. Enzymes are placed on a folded membrane organelle called the *endoplasmic reticulum*. Seeking analogues everywhere, we see that its folds resemble the folding of the small intestine. The endoplasmic reticulum is a large membrane, riddled with enzymes placed like a conveyor belt system, which folds over and over on itself like sheets of linen or filo dough.

The cellular realm does its work step by step. The system we call "digestion" follows the same plan on a macroscopic level.

REPRODUCTION, INTRACELLULAR COMMUNICATION, AND THE NUCLEUS

Every cell person has a nucleus. Most of us have heard of this. We have probably also heard that the nucleus contains our genetic code, our DNA. For biologists, the presence of a membrane-bound nucleus containing DNA actually defines a true

cell, which is known as a *"eukaryote."* (Though the more ancient types of cells or prokaryotes also have DNA, it is scattered
within them and not contained as a single organelle. We know
these ancient, prokaryotic cells today as blue-green algae.)

As for the spacesuit, the cellular prototype for both our
brains and our reproductive systems are found in the nucleus,
the DNA, the ribosomes, the cytoplasm, and their interaction.
Modesty and propriety *(blush)* dictate that I must describe the
brain first.

In the previous section, the enzymes were introduced.
These were described as complex protein molecules: chains
of amino acids linked in a specific sequence, which form a
specific shape and energy configuration, for a specific metabolic activity. *The sequence of these amino a cid molecules is the key
to their specificity!* So if the enzymes are the cell's biomolecular
splicers, and if enzymes are themselves an amino acid chain
spliced together, who splices the amino acids together to make
the enzymes?

Aha! Take a guess!

The DNA, working with its counterpart in the cytoplasm:
the RNA. DNA is a huge codebook. Embedded in its code are
the sequences for every enzyme possible in every cell of the
human spacesuit. Yet each cell person has only a portion of
that codebook activated inside it, the portions relevant to its
specific function.

What do I mean by this? For example, the gene sequence
for thyroid hormone is found in every cellular nucleus, but it is
only *activated* in the cellular community that forms the thyroid
gland. The sequence is inhibited in the DNA of all the other
cells of the body.

The DNA is a code for only those enzymes needed at

any specific moment for that particular cell person. The DNA molecule, when viewed under a light microscope, is compacted and folds in and around itself, forming what we see as *chromosomes.*

The brain, the DNA's somatic analog, folds in and around itself in a similar way, and functions in exactly the same way. It is a bundle of nerve tissue that can be described as hills of grooved and fissured layers (gross, but not so bad when grilled with butter, garlic, and lemon!). The brain is a central monitoring system. It knows what and when each activity needs to occur.

This is an elaboration of how the DNA dances in a cell. The DNA, contained in its own membrane, like the brain contained in the cranial bones of the skull, is another defining feature of "true cells", or eukaryotes (as the structure and function our brain defines *Homo sapiens.*)

DNA AND REPRODUCTION

Reproductive capacity is another feature of the cellular realm. The ability of the people of the cellular realm to replenish their own kind before they succumb to planned obsolescence (death) is an innate ability for all living entities. We call ourselves mortal because we die. However, the beings that live on Earth, and are needed by the Earth to fulfill her purpose, reproduce in order to make more of themselves so their *kind* as a collective doesn't die.

Some cell people can divide themselves into two. Way cool! Through a process called *mitosis* they go through elaborate steps to manufacture a duplicate of their DNA. Once completed, they place the duplicate in its own membrane surrounded by its own organelles and pinch themselves off to form two, generating what is sweetly known as "daughter" cells.

In the somatic realm, however, the reproduction of the human spacesuit manifests in sexual *dimorphism*, another of the possibilities in multicellular cooperation within the cellular realm. Our species is defined as a sexually dimorphic species (dimorphic = two forms: male and female.) Our reproductive organs and systems are arranged so that each "seed" of a spacesuit—either a sperm or an egg—houses only *half* a DNA molecule. The *sexual union* of spacesuits is where these two DNA halves meet, forming a new spacesuit entity.

When we look at subjects like sexuality, it's important to keep in mind its *(ids!)* purpose regarding the reproduction of the spacesuit.

EXTRACELLULAR COMMUNICATION

Let us end our discussion of the cellular realm with a mention of communication between the cell people. The last feature of eukaryotes is their ability to sense, interpret, and respond to stimulation coming from the external environment. For our spacesuits, these abilities involve organs of sensation and action that affect phenomena outside the cell as well as inside and between cells, or *intercellular communication.* This subject requires much thought and some detail to explain, as it regards our spacesuit, so I will reserve the subject for the later, where we explore the somatic and subtle energy realms of the spacesuit.

We have traveled through many, multidimensional analogues, including the mitochondria and the lungs, the DNA and the brain. Biologists describe the structures of cellular organelles as their "architectural arrangements." I can appreciate the metaphor, especially when I consider the origins of the word "cell." It comes from the Latin word *"cella,"* meaning "small room." We've reviewed most of the features of eukaryotes, which include a lipid membrane, protein enzymes, membrane-bound DNA, and carbohydrate- and oxygen-based aerobic respiration.

The functions of the body, the spacesuit, are elaborations of the features of unicellular organisms. These features define all living eukaryotes, as they participate in the dance of the elements. The spacesuit, therefore, must also embody these same features. If we only think of ourselves as amoebae, with bones and arms in the place of pseudopodia, the rest comes easy!

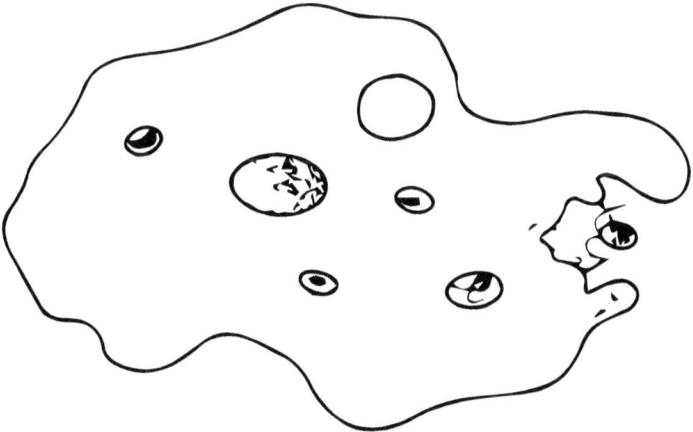

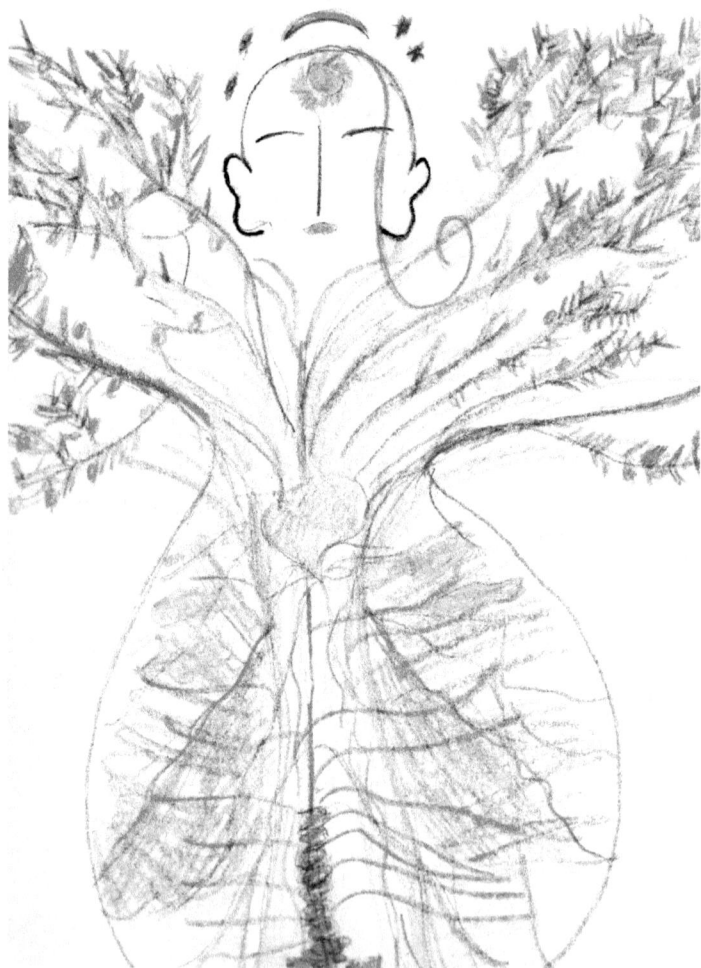

Chapter 4

The Somatic Realm

"For now we see that the functional unity of the multicellular organism is derived from the functional unity of the unicellular organism."
—Wilhelm Reich, *Sexuality and Anxiety*

Enlarge and widen your perspective. Consider the Earth, with all her elements mixing and separating, heating and cooling on her surface, covered and protected by the atmosphere. Her diverse forms of life are meeting centers for the elements to dance.

Now imagine the Earth's surface, called the *"crust,"* being like an orange peel. Watch the Earth's crust peeling itself off, away from the juicy core. Take that in both hands, and then fold the delicate surface of the Earth outside in, just like you might do with an orange peel, seal it tight, and, voila, you have a human body.

We have rivers, our circulatory vessels; mountains and stones, our bones; lakes and oceans, our extracellular fluid; and trees, our lungs. All life forms of the cellular realm in the spacesuit are covered and protected by skin.

THE SPACESUIT AS AN ECOSYSTEM

Well, here we are finally at the level of you, the level of magnification where you can see your own spacesuit in a mirror.

Thus far in our travels, we've seen the body as a container, a meeting place between the realm of the cell people, and with Earth citizens from the atomic realm transporting in and out. The spacesuit is an adaptation to the planetary forces interacting with the somatic forms. The spacesuit is also a *mirror* of those planetary forces. The human body is perfect!

Remember that people are good for plants? We're so good for plants, in fact, that our *reproductive* organs ensure there is a continuation of our species (which provides tragic-comic entertainment in our personal lives). Because the spacesuit is interactive with the environmental changes that occur on the Earth, it has evolved accordingly. The Earth, with her rotation around the Sun, itself spiraling within a galaxy, imposes her own environmental imperatives.

Now, consider our original premise that our spacesuits have yet another imperative: a soul imperative. The spirit, soul, *atman*, or whatever term you choose, is something integrated in the real world, and yet separate from the phenomena of the real world. It is described as something subtle within the denser realms, symbolized as *light with the darkness* in the Christian gospels, or the *genie in the lamp*, and other delicious metaphors from ancient cultures. And it has only one need: to be remembered!

The spacesuit, this temporary, mortal, living laboratory experiment, is the medium through which we can explore the possibilities of the soul, our electric body. Our bodies possess the means and opportunity for self-reflection. The self whispers to us, "Remember me."

So we see that in considering the somatic realm, we have much ground to cover. Let us begin by continuing the topic in the description of cellular imperatives, and the analogous somatic organ/systems that perform the necessary operations keeping the spacesuit alive. Here we will focus on sensation, perception, and action.

SENSATION, PERCEPTION, RESPONSE AND ACTION

Let us return now to the mundane attributes of the somatic realm. In so doing, let us not fall for the old trick of using the word "mundane" to indicate something trivial, irrelevant, or, worst of all, unimportant. It reveals the disrespect our times have linguistically placed on the Earth. Mundane comes from the Latin root *"mundus,"* which refers to the world—the entirety of the Earth realm. Let us imbue the word "mundane" with a deeper sense of reverence and awe for the miracle of life, Earth, and the universe.

We have explored the features that define the architecture of a true cell, which encompasses a lipid membrane, a nucleus with DNA, metabolic enzymes, reproductive capacity, and movement. The ecosystem within the spacesuit requires replenishment, as described in the previous chapter, and the imperatives of the cellular realm direct much of our energetic activities. We have also seen how the organelles of the cell people are analogous to the organ/systems of the spacesuit and the tissues that represent these features on the macrocosmic level.

Two more important features of a true cell concern *sensation* and *response*. In the cellular realm, sensation occurs on its surface: the plasma membrane. Recall this lipid, oily covering. This membrane can fold outward, forming small hair-like projections that recognize and respond to the stimuli of pressure, light, heat, or a specific molecule, be it a food or a poison. Sensation and response are two of the multiple concerns of living beings.

The spacesuit does the same thing. Neurology informs us that the human body is a *sensory driven being*, or organism. It seeks the materials it needs for its sustained life, and can recognize and differentiate food from poison, heat from cold, touch from trauma, light from dark. This recognition is automatic, as there are populations of cell people whose job it is to monitor and adjust these conditions, and allow us to know *anything*. So where do *we* come in?

When we take consciousness into consideration, our organ/systems function on two different levels. On the *cognitive* level there are the operations where we, who live in the spacesuit, actually perceive, consider, and act in a willful manner. For example, I see an apple on a tree. I want to eat that apple. I walk to the tree, pick off the apple, and eat it. (Hopefully I'm not in the Land of Oz and won't get slapped!)

On the *autonomic* level, there are operations where we have no perception, no cognition, and the responses are independent of our intentions. We know these as *autonomic responses*. For example, I have no ability to perceive how much thyroid hormone (TH) is floating around my bloodstream. But the spacesuit does! Thyroid hormone is so important that there are populations of endocrine cell people whose only job is to constantly count how much TH is floating around my bloodstream, and to make adjustments if levels get too high or too low. There are at least eight distinct populations of cells that participate in monitoring and adjusting TH. All of this sensing and adjusting occurs without my having the slightest cognitive awareness.

What I have been describing is the difference between *sensation* and *perception*. Sensation is a neuron's ability to sense a stimulus. Perception is the ability for *me* to know that a neuron is responding to a stimulus, or, in other words, to *sense* that the stimulus is affecting *me*. Thyroid hormone levels generate an electromagnetic pressure on certain neurons, which respond. These neurons sense the pressure though I don't *perceive* it!

We already saw this in an earlier chapter when we entered the swimming pool. Remember? The mechanoreceptors sensed the pressure of the water in the pool against our bodies, and for a while "reported" the new pressure information to our cognitive awareness. In time, we no longer felt (perceived) the water on the body, though the spacesuit continued to sense and monitor the pressure.

SENSORY NEURONS AND MODALITY: A RETURN TO THE CONCEPT OF DENSITY

Neurons are as permanent as this spacesuit. They don't divide to make more of themselves, anymore than "we" do. They are born, grow, and develop with our bodies, remaining intact for our whole lives. Their inner molecular machinery is constantly rebuilding itself, but the cells themselves never divide and, therefore, never do they follow the commandment: *Be fruitful and multiply.*

Skin cells, on the other hand, are constantly dividing and rebuilding our outer layers, every two weeks in fact, possibly so that we can continue to taste so good to each other! *Yum!*

The spacesuit contains five distinct populations of sensory cell people, or neurons, whom I like to think of as sensors (to use another of Mr. Spock's phrases which, as it turns out, is more accurate). These sensors convey *(Oy vay!)* information to the brain. Each type of neuron is coded for one of five specific *densities* acting on the body.

Before going on, we must make another distinction. In our common usage, we perceive and describe ourselves as possessing five *senses:* touch, taste, smell, sight, and sound. Yet, you shall soon discover that when we look at the actual cell people and what they sense, as *sensors*, we see a different and expanded version of the same story.

The following comparative table lists the sensors in order from greatest to least dense.

Neuron Sensor	Qualified Sense
Mechanoreceptor	Touch, Hearing
Chemoreceptor	Taste, Smell
Photoreceptor	Vision
Thermoreceptor	Heat/Cold
Nociceptor	Pain/Pleasure

Each *sensor* conveys only that degree of density for which it is programmed. For example: Photoreceptors only convey *light* and do not convey *touch*. This quality of a neuron, to convey only one type of signal, is called its *modality.*

The first sensor on the above list is one familiar to us: the mechanoreceptor. It is responsive to physical forces acting on the body's surface, such as someone's thumb pressing on my skin or a tic crawling up my arm. *(Yuk!)* Mechanoreceptors are the cell people who communicate touch, pressure, vibration, and, surprisingly, sound!

Sound? Did you say sound?

Yes, I did!

Sound and language are magic! The world's scriptures and mystical storytellers attest to consciousness-imbued sound being the foundation of the manifest world. It is of such a subtle nature that we have no sense organ for "sound" *per se*, like we do for light. Our ears can only sense the wave patterns of air molecules beating on our eardrums, which are interpreted and differentiated by the brain as sound, speech or noise. As mysterious as sound and thought may be, the miracle of spoken language is the prime hallmark of our species.

Speech is the result of exhaled breath moving through tunnels formed by the throat, tongue, and mouth. We consciously learn how to shape those tunnels as children. Once exhaled, the air, whose molecules are now "shaped" by the speech, travels through the atmosphere to the ear tunnels of a listener. *Consciousness* and *meaning* are embodied in the vibration carried by the air that carries a spoken word, like a radio wave. Once the waves enter the listener's ear, they vibrate a skin-covered window called the *"eardrum,"* causing it to vibrate, just like speakers in a sound system vibrate when playing a CD.

This vibratory wave is amplified by the eardrum, and then passes through a liquid tube, whose inner lining is filled with *micro-hairs.* Each of these tiny hairs is connected to a *mechanore-*

ceptor, and when the passing wave moves the hair, it signals the brain. What we *hear* is actually the brain's recognition of these vibratory patterns as they trigger little hairs.

There is no human sense of sound. Sound's presence is determined by sensors of the greatest densities of experience, the mechanoreceptors!

The next group of sensors, the *chemoreceptors,* responds to specific biochemical entities in the atomic realm, entities less dense than those that trigger touch. Chemoreceptors are the cell people who count thyroid hormone or receive chemical messages from other cell people. We have two of our five physical senses connected to this second type of neuron: our senses of smell and of taste. Molecules and ions have a specific shape and form, and the plasma membranes of these sensors have micro-organs embedded on the surface that fit specific molecules. It's a lock and key system, where the plasma membrane is the keyhole while the molecule is the key.

Every cell has its own coded set of "keyholes," which are called *receptors* in the life sciences. This is especially true for the cell people in the neuroendocrine system. Some receptors are limited to a small population of cells, like those that count thyroid hormone molecules. Other receptors are universal, like the keyhole for insulin, which allows glucose molecules to enter all the cells for the purpose of aerobic respiration, which is how they get energy. In our nose and on our tongue, chemoreceptors are the cell people that inform us of what we taste and smell.

Okay, so that's four of our physical senses governed by only two types of sensors!

The third type of sensor on our list, a *photoreceptor,* is responsive to electromagnetic waves within a specific range of the light spectrum. Vision is possible because populations of cell people play with their electric membranes in response to specific waves of color-refracted light. They work like a prism, or like the lens of a camera, and are responsive to specific colors called "primary" (red, blue, yellow, and green).

When we include our vision sense, we see that what we call our five senses are the result of the lives of only three types of sensory neurons. So what else can we sense?

Recognition of states of cold, hot and "just right" are *thermal* senses. Our sensors that respond to changes in temperature and inform the brain accordingly are *thermoreceptors*. We are not in the habit of considering temperature a sense, yet we know it when it is out of balance, for our range is limited. That is why shelter seeking and home maintenance occupies so much of our time. We also recognize it in each other when we say, "She's such a cold person" or "He's hot!" or even "Her singing warms my soul!" Yet, most of us don't think of thermal recognition as a sense.

As for our fifth sensor, I have used the term *"intuitive sense"* in the list. Science sees it otherwise—and herein lies a problem. The neurons responsible for this sense are *nociceptors*. In our culture, their effect has been defined as the "sense" of pain. But this explains only half the story.

As it turns out, the sense of pain exists within a pain/pleasure binary system encoded in the brain for the purpose of learning anything on this plane of consciousness. It's called the *limbic system*. In fact, in order for a "thing" to enter our conscious mind at all, it must possess a stimulus strong enough to pass through the neurological community of the limbic system.

Nociceptors offer us a continuum of blended perceptions

that result in the entirety of our emotional expression. The spectrum concerns love and trust on one end, fear and rage on the other, and everything else in between. Feelings aren't made up. They are already encoded in our spacesuit. We *learn* what triggers them through the waves of different experiences we term painful or pleasurable. And to think we rarely consider this ability a sense!

WILLFUL ACTION AND MOTOR RESPONSE

The five sensors create a mosaic hologram of what we perceive as reality. We seek and act on conscious and subconscious levels, satisfying the needs of our spacesuit, the cells, and the planet. Although our actions are complex and multimodal, they still occur within the framework of what our collection of sensors can recognize.

So we travel in our spacesuits to and from bioregional ecosystems in order to reach places where we manipulate the environment in order to satisfy the spacesuit's need for balance in its internal ecosystem. We make willful, preferential choices, and the spacesuit responds with *actions*, some learned, some reflexive: what the life scientists call *motor responses.*

For our spacesuit, action amounts to only two possible motor responses: contraction of muscles and secretion of glands. That's it! *Everything we say we do and feel is the expression of a specific combination of moment-by-moment contractions and secretions.*

In using the word "combination," I mean a *huge* combination: complex and coordinated with precise sequencing, timing, and supportive activity. For example: say I want to exercise my right arm with a twenty-five-pound free weight. I'm sitting in a chair looking at the weight while focusing on my beginning posture. At this moment, the simple act of imagining sets off the brain, which prepares the contraction sequences I'm planning. After lifting the weight, I begin to pump my biceps muscle. The brain is now informed of actual changes in stress on the elbow joint, and tells the *biceps brachii* muscle to engage more muscle cell people to accommodate the new physical forces being exerted on the joints. This continues until the elbow joint relaxes.

At the same time *I'm* focusing on my arm, pumping and counting, the rest of my spacesuit is supporting the activity. The increased amount of work being done requires more oxygen, so the brain simultaneously instructs the blood vessels in the shoulder and arm regions to constrict, causing increased pressure. This pressure accelerates the regional flow of blood, and now more oxygen is delivered to the region at a faster rate. The brain also signals the lungs to breathe deeper and faster, again increasing the oxygen levels. Finally, the adrenal glands secrete adrenaline, which increases the rates of both the heart and lungs.

In the musculoskeletal world, while the arm is pumping, the hip, back, and abdominal muscles are keeping me from tilting and maintaining my relationship with gravity: both activities are *subconscious movements*. Different parts of the brain direct these regions simultaneously, *supporting the activity that has my attention at any moment.*

In my mind, all I'm doing is pumping a free weight. In the collective mind of the spacesuit, everything else I described and so much more has captured its attention! Everything we say we do manifests as contraction and secretion patterns.

Compare this complexity to its prototype: the simple pulsation and motion of a unicellular organism. Remember? The cytoskeleton, a network of charged, protein fibers slid over itself, and the cell simply pulsed, while the plasma membrane was capable of moving hairs and tails on its surface, allowing it to glide through air and water. The spacesuit's elaboration of this prototype consumes huge amounts of energy by the organs we know as the neuromuscular system. Our spacesuit has both complicated and condensed the features of true cells.

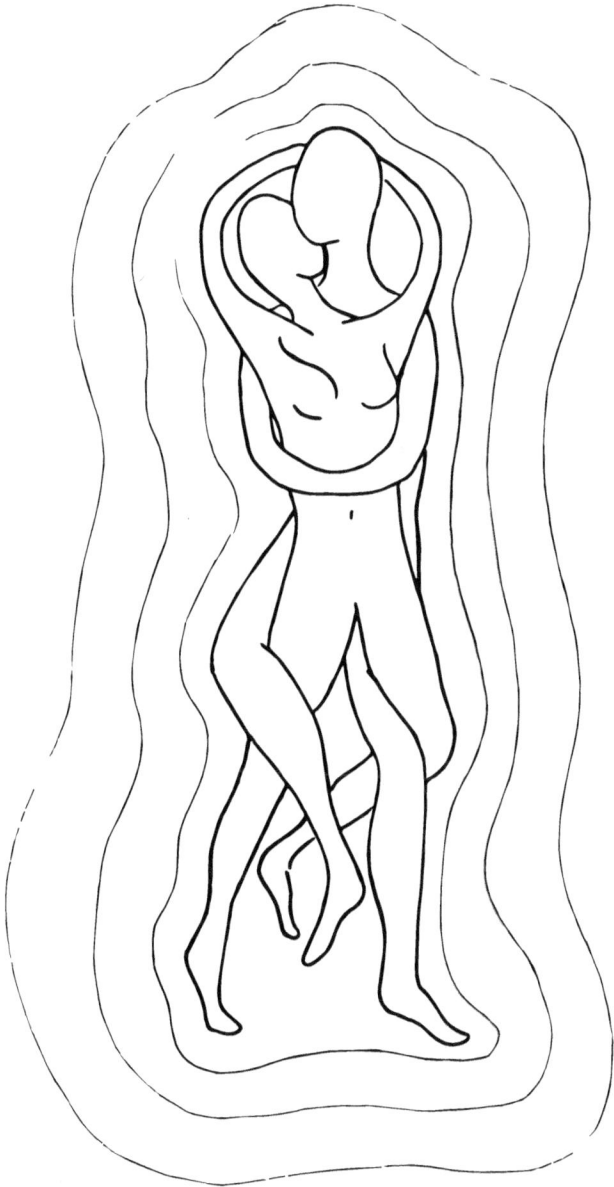

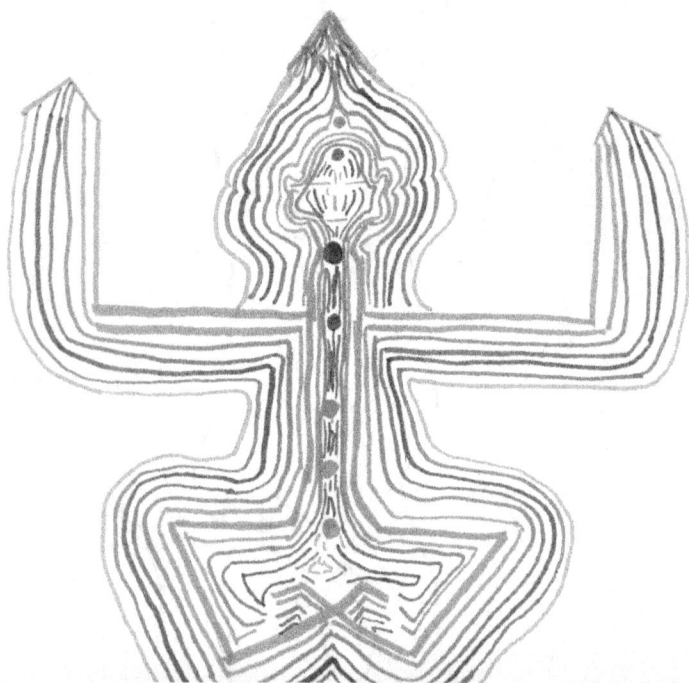

Chapter 5

The Subtle Realm:

Central and Peripheral Channels

Consider the spine. Imagine you are standing, your leg and back muscles pushing against a gravitational force that pulls you down. Imagine a plumb line of circulating energy, drawn from your tailbone up through the center of your spine, through your neck, then upward through your skull. You've just traversed the *central channels*.

This stream of energy is perpendicular to the Earth's surface, and parallel to the forces of gravity. The central channels are spoken of as the source of consciousness, feeling, and power within, which is directly linked to the subtle realms outside the spacesuit and provide connection with the body's periphery.

The force of the central channels impels the spacesuit to stand upright. The spine reaches upward, and the rest of the body (the periphery) accommodates that center. The spine is the center of the subtle energy body and physiology agrees: The point just a couple inches in front of our tailbone (sacrum) is our physiological center of gravity The spacesuit, in both the somatic and subtle realms, is consistent in its metaphoric analogy.

SUBTLE ENERGY: ANATOMY AND PHYSIOLOGY

We have thus far considered the nature of the universe as imitation, multiplication, and condensation. We've seen how the different realms of magnification share metaphoric analogs with each other. The atom and the Solar System, the cell and the spacesuit mirror each other in form and function. They embody the principle of cooperation within a universe of complementary opposites. If this is true for the material realms, why is it not also true for the subtle realm? Wouldn't the spacesuit, which houses the subtle body, mirror the structure, form, and function of the subtle body's electromagnetic possibilities, just as it does for the cell?

My best guess: Of course it does!

We've explored how our physical bodies, these somatic spacesuits, are a crossroad between the realms of the Earth and cell, the cell being the *mini-spacesuit* within which the atomic realm can dance. We've also seen how the imperatives of the simultaneous realms of atom, molecule, and body direct most of our willful activity. Yet, the spirit realm is something both integrated and separate from all of this, something subtle within the denser realms. In Western religious traditions, this is symbolized as *light within the darkness*. It, too, demands of us, "Know me!"

There is a difference: The soul *whispers*, while the real world *screams*.

The subtlety of this realm begs certain questions: Can our somatic spacesuit function as a medium through which we can explore the possibilities of knowing the "invisible" soul, the electric, subtle body within the spirit realm? What might the structure of the subtle body—its form, its manifestations on the somatic realm—look like?

It is from the ancient healing arts and mystical traditions that we learn the clues from which we can access, and, not surprisingly, see that mirrors and metaphors do in fact exist in our somatic perception, and have been known to exist for a long time. The Great Ones have taught us to acquaint ourselves with ourselves, to *"know thyself."*

A HISTORICAL ASIDE

In the United States, the disciplines of yoga, meridian therapy, and acupuncture are recognized by the academic traditions and practical arts of Western medicine. Yet, this is only a recent achievement. The famous visit to China by President Richard Nixon in the early 1970s generated an opening of culture and exchange from which we're still reeling. It was during this visit that a U.S. journalist underwent emergency surgery, and, instead of anesthesia, acupuncture was used. Up to that point, in the U.S. acupuncture was relegated to superstition at best, and at worst, devil worship. In spite of this official stance, it was still sought after—as folk medicines always are—by citizens in local communities across the nation where a traditional practitioner could be found in a Chinatown.

After the events of the 1972 China visit, traditional Chinese medicine (TCM), which incorporates herbs, acupuncture, and meridian therapy in its roster of practices, became an accepted study in United States institutions and legal to practice. The energy framework with which meridian therapists work gives us a map of the electromagnetic currents of energy whichcirculate throughout the body. Opening up our culture to TCM set a precedent that has since branched out to other traditions of medicine drawn from all of the former colonies of Asia.

On an equally large scale, the disciplines of Yoga, Buddhism, and martial arts furthered our understanding of the subtle realm: From these sources come pranayama, qigong, and meditation. The Beatles set the stage for yoga practice in North America, though there had been precedents, like the Transcendentalists in New England. Previously limited to urban intelligentsia and cosmopolitans, yoga went mass media with the Beatles. Bruce Lee presented the magical martial art of kung fu to the movie going world. After him, the concept of the sacred warrior exploded in our national consciousness.

At this point, it's not unreasonable to ask: How can this be? How can the surface of the body communicate with the inner body? We may ask ourselves this question as bodyworkers or as yoga and qigong students. The answer, or at least a clue, lies in our embryological origins. Without getting into detail just yet, it turns out that the entire brain, spinal cord, and peripheral nerves derive from the *same embryonic, primary germ layer as the outer layers of our skin, the epidermis.* (Remember this old joke? "Your epidermis is showing!" When was that funny, around eight years old?)

Think about it again: The brain and nervous system derive from the skin. How cool is that? This is such an important fact for bodywork therapists to grasp fully, because it explains the connection of the skin to the entire nervous system, and from there, to the entire spacesuit. It helps to explain, for example, how regular massage produces the incredible phenomenon of increased growth rate for infants born prematurely.

So let's take a short detour and visit the gestating embryo with its *three primary germ layers*.

PRIMARY GERM LAYERS

About three weeks after fertilization takes place, each of us became an embryo. At this time we look like a tiny, flat, pancake drop, three layers thick. The primary germ layers, all wrapped in a small cellular sac, are embedded in the walls of some wonderful woman's uterus at this stage of life. The layers are described as the inner, the middle, and the outer layers. The inner layer *(endoderm)* sits on a pool of nutrients called the *primitive yolk sac.* (Yup, just like a chicken egg yolk.) This inner layer absorbs food for the developing spacesuit being until it connects with the mother's blood system for nutrients. Once the blood connection is made the spacesuit person is no longer called an embryo; it is called a *fetus.*

As the spacesuit person completes gestation, that same inner, absorptive endoderm will proliferate into the entire gastrointestinal tract, the single tube that begins at the mouth and ends at the anus, continuing through our lives in its absorptive capacity already present at the beginning.

How beautiful!

The outer layer *(ectoderm)* covers the embryo as it develops, and continues in this function as it becomes the epidermis, the outermost layer of the skin. But then a truly amazing thing happens. This same layer begins a *longitudinal fold* (actually called the *"primitive groove"*) into the middle layer, loops back, pinches/closes off, and becomes the entire nervous system, complete with a hole in its center from the brain to the spinal cord. This tube is lined with ectoderm, which will grow into the cells that make cerebrospinal fluid. The connection between what will become the skin and the brain/spinal cord is thorough and complete.

Again, how beautiful!

The middle layer *(mesoderm)* becomes everything else: organs, muscle, blood vessels, lungs, heart, tendons, ligaments, and bones—everything. (Well, just about everything!) The mesoderm tissues immediately surrounding the now-pinched off ectoderm/nervous system become the meninges, the bones that surround and protect the region, the muscles, tendons, and ligaments that move the bones, and also the blood and lymph vessels that feed all the cell people.

Voila! You and me!

Come now, really, is this not incredibly beautiful?

ENERGY

The traditions of the East inform us of a subtle energy body, consisting of streams of subtle energy *particles* that run along the surface of the body, up and down the spine, and throughout the internal structures of the spacesuit. Some channels can be accessed by the mind and willful concentration in the form of meditation, prayer, breath, chanting, and physical practices, like yoga, tai chi, and dance. Others are accessed by herbal medicines or passive bodywork therapies, among them touch, oils, needles, sound, and light.

The channels conduct the flow of primal energy particles called *"chi"* by the Chinese and *"prana"* by the Indians. Yoga philosophy attributes three qualities to this primal energy: existence *(sat)*, consciousness *(chit)*, and the added component of emotion: joy/bliss *(ananda)*. This, by the way, is a truly amazing concept, linking particulate matter with both *mind* and *feeling*. It is consistent with the discoveries of our era, for this same conclusion has been reached by quantum physicists.

Oriental traditions describe three aspects of the *subtle energy body*: the spinal or axial/central currents *(sushumna, ida, and pingala)*, the peripheral currents *(meridians, nadis, sen lines)*, and seven energy centers known as *chakras*. Each aspect of the subtle realm displays the same properties we've been observing throughout the rest of our exploration. Ours is a universe of complementary opposed forces resolved by the principle of cooperation. The subtle energy realm is no exception. This chapter will focus on the central and peripheral channels of the energy body, while the seven energy centers, the chakras, will be explored in the next chapter.

SUBTLE ANATOMY

When I imagine currents of subtle energy, I begin by thinking about electricity. A *current* of electricity is familiar to us as a force that runs along a wire from some power source to some appliance or electrical apparatus. We can almost imagine *it* moving from pole A to pole B. And it goes without saying that anyone who has been shocked by an electric current certainly knows electricity on a personal, somatic level.

Yet when we talk to electrical engineers like my uncle (who was very helpful to me in understanding electricity, by the way) about this current, what they describe as electricity is in fact a *dual, complementary opposing motion*. As it turns out, what we call electricity is described as the simultaneous movement of an *electron* from pole A to pole B in one direction, complemented by a *proton* moving from pole B to pole A in an equal and opposite direction. This phenomenon of equal and opposite streams of energy manifests in both the subtle and somatic realms, for the universe is *relatively* consistent on every level.

Okay, let's build an energy body. As a starting point, we'll shift our magnification to the cellular realm of the spacesuit, inhabited by the little cell people who form the somatic organ systems of tubes and sacks. As we've seen, every cell person has, among other properties, an *electrical nature*, making each cell an *electromagnetic unit*. This is possible because ions flow in and out of each cell, maintaining a steady state *voltage* across its membrane. Recall that the cell lives in an Everglades-like tissue-fluid, a pool of nutrients having an electrical property of its own. Remember also that the activities of cell populations are *responses* determined either by the constituents of the extracellular fluid, or modified by electrical stimulation by neurons.

Now shift again, enlarge and think of the organ systems. Each tube of the spacesuit's organic systems, comprised of populations of electrified cellular units, conducts an *electrically charged fluid*, be it blood, food in the gastrointestinal (GI) tract, or cerebrospinal fluid. If we visualize the movement of different electrified fluids as currents of energy, then we are closer to being able to see the mirror that the subtle realm displays in both location and in function. The electrified cell people, living in an electrified ecosystem, join in some form with others, and generate an electrified tube system that conducts electric fluids.

Energy currents flow in multiple dimensions throughout the organ systems. Waves of electrical current flow along the walls of the muscle-lined tube in—say, the GI tract— generating a stream of nervous and muscle energy that moves in a downward direction as the tube squeezes slowly and sequentially along the entire tract segment by segment, like a snake swallowing an elephant. (If you are a fan of *The Little Prince* by Antoine de Saint-Exupéry, about a prince who hasn't as yet become a grownup, you'll recognize this image. If you aren't, please read. The pictures are a joy to behold.)

All the squeezing contractions along the GI tube are preceded by electrical shocks that come from neurons. The neurons *time* the contractions like the old-style distributors in automobiles used to time the firing of spark plugs: in a specific sequence.

So we have four simultaneous currents:

1. A wave of subtle, nerve energy moves down a population of neuron *"wires"* and,
2. *"Shocks"* the already electrified GI tube, made of
3. Electrified *cells,* conducting
4. An electrified *fluid* in a downward direction.

Close your eyes a moment and see if you can see it magnification by magnification.

Let's review one more time: In the example just given, we looked at one cell person, itself electrical, with current moving all around its *"skin,"* or lipid-rich cell membrane. At the same time we saw the cell living in a pool of charged particles, an ecosystem with electric potentiality. This pool surrounds the cell's charged membrane. Also, we imagined a nerve fiber *from above* bringing a charge of electric current to the membrane of the cell, affecting its electric state, driving that cell either to contraction, relaxation, or secretion. Hence, three categories of electric fields are in motion all in one moment.

Finally, we imagined the electric fluid—the food we swallow—traveling down this same tube and manifesting an electric current.

Those are the only four currents I talked about. There are others. Yet, always remember: The prototype is the cell itself, electrical in nature, composed of atoms and molecules themselves electrical in nature. Together they are one, big, electrical family!

TRANSPARENCIES AND OVERHEAD PROJECTORS

Now we are in a place where we can imagine an overlapping—or rather a superimposing —of bodies, one comprised of subtle energy, the other comprised of a denser, physical substance, manifesting as living, electrified, tube-forming cell people, themselves layered in an inner ocean of electrified extracellular fluids. Like a set of transparencies placed one over another on an overhead projector, we can view our subtle energy realm within the very fabric of the physical, or somatic, realm.

The subtle energy realm is always present. It's just a question of what realm is represented when a transparency is visualized or placed over another. If we imagine the streams and currents as light, it allows us indefinite amounts of playful, imaginary association with transparencies. What follows is an offering, a sampling of possibilities.

PERIPHERAL CHANNELS: FUN WITH MERIDIANS/NADIS

Traditional Chinese medicine, ayurveda, Thai massage, and shiatsu constitute a sample of therapies from around the world that work through the *peripheral channels,* which conduct subtle energy currents *up the front* and *down the back* of the body. These channels are referred to as *meridians, nadis,* and *sen lines,* among other things.

The description up the front/down the back, when used in an Asian context, implies a person standing with his or her arms overhead, palms facing forward.

Located along the course of each meridian are *points* where energies can get blocked, not unlike a logjam in a river, where the water upstream has greater force than downstream from the logjam. The same dynamics apply to the points as they do a logjam, where energies are increased on one side of the blockage, while weakened on the other, requiring sedating and tonifying treatments, respectively. Point therapies that work with these blockages include the introduction of metal or wood elements (needles), heated herbs (moxibustion), oils (aromatherapy), or touch therapies (massage). The above-mentioned therapies are familiar to many of us.

So let's have some fun with transparencies! As a starting point, take the wrist and forearm as an example, for here we see a rather perfect instance of complementary energies traveling tandem. There are *three* meridians located on the front *(anterior)* of the wrist, and *three* on the back *(posterior)*. The direction of the flow of energy is complementary. The front of the arm conducts energy from the forearm down towards the fingers, while in the back of the wrist the meridian energy is conducted from the fingers through the wrist to the shoulder.

And so we have a first transparency layer, a mapping of subtle energies flowing in complementary/ opposing directions on the front and back of the arm.

Can you see it? Stop a moment and try.

How is this mirrored on the somatic realm? The life sciences observe three types of vessels found in the wrist: arteries, veins, and nerves. The vessels are named, starting from the thumb side, the radial, medial, and ulnar, be they arteries, veins, or nerves. (The general rule followed in naming blood vessels and nerves is that they are named after the bone or skeletal region over which they are found. Thus, the radial artery, vein, and nerve are found on the side of the forearm where the bone called the "radius" is located.)

Now consider *location and depth*. When you look at the front of your wrist, can you see the dark, blood vessels there? Those vessels are the veins. Veins are the blood vessels closest to the skin, which is really smart. If we get a superficial cut, the slowest moving blood vessel is closest to the skin, not the faster artery.

Now think a little deeper. The three arteries lie *underneath* the three veins. And when you go even deeper, you find the three nerves lying even deeper. The nerves are all bundled together, the arteries and veins are bundled together, and finally, the whole mess is bundled together. It is a perfect organization. *Amen!*

Now consider *direction of energy flow*. Each of the three arteries are conducting blood from the arm to the fingers, while the veins are conducting blood from the fingers to the shoulder or chest, just like the meridians! If we transform the image of blood as a fluid into the image of electrical, liquid light, then we can view a stream of energy that travels in vessels within the body, approximating the locations of the meridian energies. Blood moves in energy streams that are analogous to our transparencies of the meridians. The arterial stream and venous stream together form a complementary/opposing circulation in tandem.

Let's add another somatic realm transparency to this image: the nerves of the wrist. The nerve signals stream out of and into the spinal cord through three different bundles of nerves, the radial, median, and ulnar nerves. Each nerve is a bundle of Inspector Gadget-like "limbs" or wires *(axons)* that conduct a pattern of electrical signals. The signals are, once again, found traveling in complementary/opposing directions!

On the one hand (pardon the pun) the sensory neurons conduct signals from the fingers to the wrist, up the arm, and to the spinal cord and brain. The motor neurons conduct signals from the brain and spinal cord to the hand. These two opposing movements of current, conducted along the membranes of neuron axons, are located and *bundled together* in tandem. This can be compared to telephone wires, conducting signals to and from your home, all bundled together.

So we see multiple energy streams in the limbs and in the core of our spacesuit. We see subtle energy streams in the meridians and nadis. On the physical plane, we can see their somatic counterparts, energy streams in the form of electrical fluids and nerve currents, moving through the organ systems of the somatic realm.

There are twelve meridians in the acupuncture system, and each is associated with an organ/system. Six of the meridians travel up the front of the body, while the other six travel down the back of the body. The subtle realm is here depicted as possessing the qualities of both *motion* and complementary *direction*. (In physics, motion in a specific direction is called a *vector.*)

Yet another anatomical mirror of the subtle meridian system is available to us in the somatic realm of the spacesuit, for each of the twelve peripheral meridians have a connecting point on one of the twelve thoracic vertebrae. In other words, the meridians—that is, the entire subtle energy system—can be accessed from these vertebrae. What is fascinating here is the meridian system's relevance to neurology, for the placement of the cell bodies that comprise the sympathetic nervous system (fight-or-flight) is found only in the thoracic segments of the spine. The nerves exit a hole *(foramen)* between the vertebrae and, from here, connect with every tissue in the body.

Are you impressed with yourself yet? I certainly am!

CENTRAL CHANNELS: BONES, BRAINS, AND NEURON BUNDLES

The life sciences perceive the spacesuit's spinal region as a *central axis,* and group the relevant bones as the *axial skeleton.* It includes the bones of the spine—the vertebrae, sacrum, and coccyx—and the bones of the skull. Further, the axial skeleton houses and protects the brain and spinal cord, which are wrapped in an airtight, three-layered connective tissue sac called the *"meninges."* (You've actually heard of these: They're the tissues that get sick when you have something called *meningitis.*) The meninges are filled with a thick fluid, the *cerebrospinal fluid,* which fills up the entire space between the sack and the brain/spinal cord. This cushions the neurons, and prevents them from banging against the inner walls of the spine or skull.

Most of us are familiar with the brain. We know it as the

central control region of our spacesuit. The brain receives and processes incomprehensible amounts of information/bytes. It "decides" what it all means and then responds in whatever ways it deems appropriate. It informs us of our options.

The spinal cord, descending from the brain, serves two major functions in the spacesuit. Its first function is to be an *electrical roadway*, an "interstate highway" for cellular communication. As such, it conveys sensory information (the latest news) from the rest of the body (the periphery) up the back of the cord to the brain, while simultaneously conveying responses (orders) from the brain down the front of the cord. Notice the direction of electrical nerve energy in the cord. Sensory information travels *up the back* of the spinal cord *to* the brain, while motor information travels *down the front* of the spinal cord *from* the brain.

The second function of the spinal cord involves the muscle systems that move bones and organs. If you look at a cross section of the spinal cord, you'll see an H-shaped area in the center that appears relatively gray, surrounded by areas that are relatively white. The gray area is the home of the *nerve cell people* who are the direct link to the muscles and glands of the spacesuit.

Remember that the voluntary muscle cell people only contract when they receive a command to contract from the neuron cell people, whose bodies live in the gray matter of spinal cord. Remember also that their axons, or "wires," grow out from this region of the cord (*à la* Inspector Gadget) to the developed shoulder, foot, liver or whatever.

Varieties of images exist providing a sense of the subtle energy moving through the central channels. In the ayurvedic traditions of India, the central channel is called the *"sushum-*

na." Its energy travels up and down the spine and is accompanied by the two interweaving snake-like streams of the *ida* and the *pingala*. In *tantric* mystical representations, the subtle energy—*kundalini*—is presented as a coiled snake seated at the base of our spine. When activated by mystic practices, the subtle energy uncoils and rises up the spine, until it connects with centers in the skull, at which point an ecstatic state of oneness ensues. The two poles are known as *"purusha"* and *"prakriti"* in Indian traditions.

There is a neurological analog in the somatic realm of our spacesuit corresponding to the two poles: the *parasympathetic nervous system*. (We have already met its counterpart, the sympathetic nervous system, while describing the peripheral energy system in the previous section.) Like the poles of kundalini energy, one in the skull and one in the base of the spine, the parasympathetic nerve cell people live in the same polar relation to the rest of the body. One group lives in the base of the skull in the region of the brain stem that houses the *vagus nerve*, while the rest live in the *sacral* segments of the spinal cord—in other words, in the region of the lower back. The centers of the parasympathetic nervous system physically mirror the two poles of the central energy channels.

The parasympathetic cell people in the skull cluster in a part of the brain called the *"medulla oblongata."* This is located at the base of the skull where it meets the spine. If you flex your head forward, you can feel a space between the skull and neck, and that mushy stuff you're pushing on is the medulla oblongata. Cool! (And yes, I know, this is a little bit creepy, too!) The "wires" that extend from this population of neurons supply the entire spacesuit down to the navel area.

The lower, sacral "wires" supply the remaining regions of

body below the navel.

Can you imagine a flow of warm, comforting energy originating in your skull and spreading in waves, everywhere, down to the waist, while at the base of your body, your core streams the same warm energy down your lower abdomen and legs, all the way to your toes. *Mmmm.*

In the contemporary West, we don't hear much about the central channels, but our ancients have given us clues. It is no coincidence that the area at the base of the spine contains a large bone that was known as for something sacred, for they called it the *"sacrum,"* which we still do today. The Roman anatomists took their cue from the Greeks, who also named it the "holy" bone: *ieron.*

There are hints regarding central channels in the biblical story of Jacob's revelation, where waves or currents of energy were seen as angels moving *up and down a ladder.* Similarly, in the Book of the Revelation, John *heard* the energy streams as a rumbling *behind* him, causing him to turn and *see things.* Using words like "seen" and "heard," the ancients give testimony to the fact that we can and do perceive energy.

The traditions of East and West are consistent, in that it is within and through the axial skeleton that *pranic currents* travel up and down the spine, from coccyx to skull, accompanied by interweaving currents traveling up and crisscrossing along its axis. This image is actually quite familiar to us from the symbol that represents Western medicine. Taken from Ancient Greece and Rome, the *caduceus* of the God Hermes is a central rod with interweaving snakes!

You see? Descriptions of the subtle energy system abound throughout the world's mystical and poetic traditions, even if we don't always immediately know what the symbols mean.

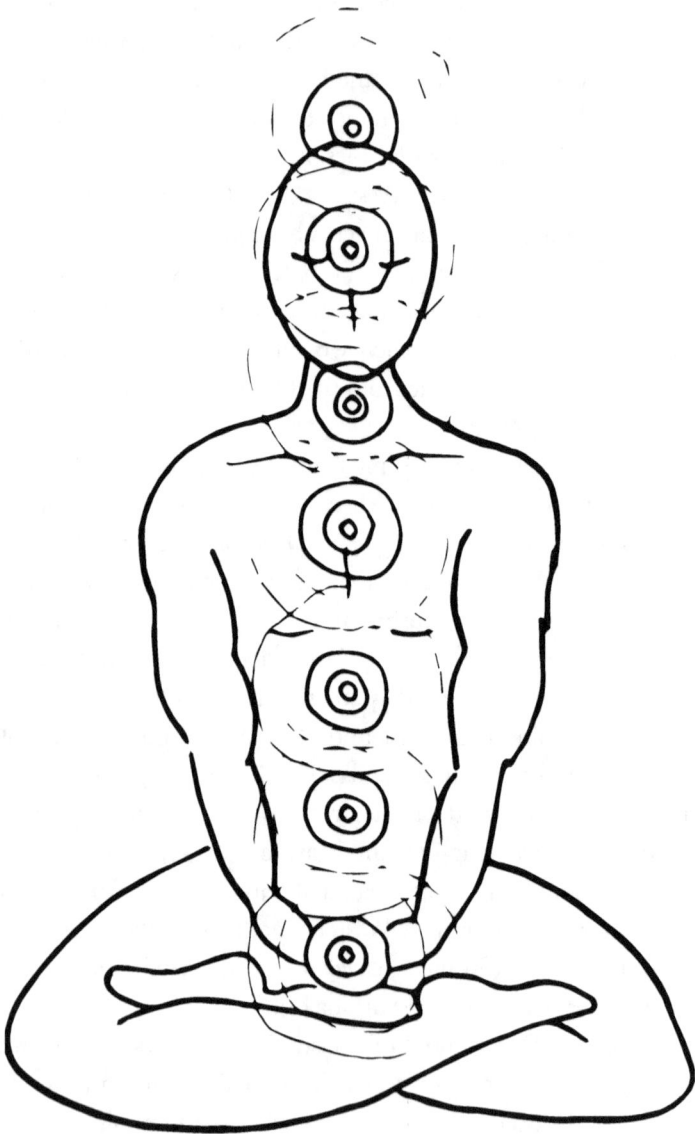

Chapter 6

The Subtle Realm

The Chakras and Endocrine Glands

"The Master of the Universe gives us glimpses, only glimpses.
It is for us to open our eyes wide."
—Chaim Potok, *My Name is Asher Lev*

In a seated, relaxed posture, recall the central channels from the last chapter: See the line of force from your coccyx and sacrum to the lumbar, thorax, and cervical regions, and on up to the top of your skull. This is your central axis.

Now imagine seven stars located in front of, and along each region of this axis. These stars are numbered one to seven, from the first star at the bottom of your spine to the seventh star at the crown of your head on top of your skull. Each radiates a liquid light.

Imagine a stream of deep purple, liquid light that radiates from this seventh star forward, loops down through the front of your body and back up through the back of your body to the fifth star located in your throat. From here, it continues up the central channel to the seventh star. Again and again, watch the seventh star send a stream of conscious light to the fifth star, and up again through the axis.

Now view the seventh star send a stream of light down and through the chest, the fourth star, and back up the central axis. Then see another stream of light sent from the seventh star through the third star in the upper abdomen and back up. Then see another sent through the second star in the lower abdomen. Finally, see light being sent through the first star the tail bone (coccyx) at the base of the spine. (If you like, you can play with each star. Their locations will be more familiar at the end of this chapter, so I thought that starting with a few "stitches" would be enough for now.)

Your body's inner, subtle realms are vibrating and weaving you an energetic rainbow self, like Joseph's cloak of many-colors described in the Torah.

THE SEVEN CHAKRAS: WHORLS OF ENERGY

In the previous chapter, we practiced visualizing streams of liquid light, currents of energy flowing through various tubes: meridians, neurons, and the fluids of blood in vessels and food in the GI tract. The tubes are continuous, and the density of fluid makes the image easier to see with our inner vision.

Visualization and inner vision, you see? We do know a little something about the subtle realms. We speak of it when discussing dreams. We view it in our imagination *(image-in-ation)*. We even feel it as a vibration between ourselves and others.

The chakras represent a different kind of energy organization than the central channels do. The Sanskrit word *"chakra"* means "wheel." The subtle energy chakras are perceived as whorls of prana, differentiated and condensed consciousness floating through the waters of the spacesuit, conveying a message, a directive, an instruction from a higher source to some distant cellular population. The chakras are strikingly mirrored in the spacesuit by their physical counterparts, the *endocrine glands,* which are the centers of our global hormonal system.

The chakras are seven in number, as are the endocrine glands. Both chakras and endocrine glands are located along the central axis of the body and associated with the spinal regions: the coccyx, the sacrum, the lumbar spine, the thorax, the cervical spine, the skull, and the crown of the head. Beginning from the bottom, here are the names of the chakras.

1. *Muladhara:* the root chakra (coccyx)
2. *Swadhisthana:* the sacral chakra (sacrum)
3. *Manipura:* the solar plexus chakra (lumbar)
4. *Anahata:* the heart chakra (thoracic)
5. *Vishuddha:* the throat chakra (throat)
6. *Ajna:* the brow chakra (cranial), also known as the "third eye"
7. *Sahasrara:* the crown chakra (area that is the "soft spot" of a newborn)

In the previous chapter, we saw that the central channels of the spine are regions of concentrated energy, much like an electric plant that generates and stores huge amounts of energy. The crown chakra is the source of this energy. Like the movement of electricity through a sequence of transformers, subtle energy is transmitted down through the central axis and dispersed out to the chakras (and peripheral channels) from this central "energy plant."

Now, the subtle realm speaks in a language that is softer, less dense, and less intense than the more manifest realms. We can "hear" it mirrored in the cellular realm in the way the cell people speak to each other in the language of *hormones*. The endocrine glands of the cellular realm generate a biomolecular stream of hormones that flow within the fluid currents of the blood, a stream within a stream of consciousness telling the cell people what to do. Blood carries everything everywhere and the biomolecule called a "hormone" is a message, a very simple message or imperative sent to some distant cell population, informing them either to turn on or turn off some aspect of their "machinery."

The first three chakras are concerned with the denser realms of food, water, and the reproduction of new spacesuit people. Their combined actions draw in and process the Earth elements, *absorbing* (feeding) and distributing those elements to the ecosystems of the spacesuit, and returning unabsorbed food back to the Earth, participating in the plant fertilization cycle. The three lower centers communicate *upward* to the heart and higher centers.

The upper three chakras are connected to the more subtle realms of air, mind, and spirit. They communicate *downward,* through the heart, and out to the periphery of the body.

At the fourth chakra, the heart chakra, the streams of the upper and lower chakras meet. The heart chakra is the energetic and systemic crossroads.

Each chakra is associated with a color, a sound, and a sphere of influence. Like the Indian *devas* (supernatural beings) and Greek gods, they have control over some aspect or quality of our lives. Let us visit each chakra and its corresponding endocrine center, and consider its location and quality, while we also visualize its colorful stream flowing through the blood.

The corresponding endocrine populations communicate through *hormones* circulating the entirety of the spacesuit, conveyed through the bloodstream—the waters—of the somatic realm. Each hormone vibrates at its own rate, generating a "sound" that permeates the fluid, giving "voice" to our seven-shaded light streams.

1. MULADHARA: KIDNEYS AND ADRENAL GLANDS

The *muladhara chakra,* located at the base of the spine in the region of the coccyx bone, is described as the source of our instincts for survival, as well the place for elimination or, as I prefer, *delivery.* For even as we eliminate substances from our bodies, we return (deliver) them back to the Earth in a new form, processed by our metabolic systems, and made available and palatable for the plants that keep us breathing.

On the level of consciousness, the root chakra is the place of our earliest differentiation: We are full or empty, moist or dry, safe or frightened, peaceful or enraged. These senses work within the regions of the brain that are the limbic system.

The root chakra, sitting at the base of the spine near the coccyx, is mirrored in its somatic analogues: the kidneys and adrenal glands. The atomic realms of the spacesuit have entrusted the kidneys with the balancing of water, pH, salinity, and protein excretion. Kidneys purify the waters of the body on an average of seventy times per day. Water is the primeval ocean of life, the medium within which our bodies are formed. Thus it seems poetically appropriate that the organs associated with the first chakra would be concerned with the very same waters from which our spacesuit arises.

Recall again that the internal environment is an Everglades-like ecosystem, whose waters must be maintained in quantity, temperature, and pressure. The kidneys see to it that the basic ions, volume, and pH of the spacesuit's waters remain in balance, while the endocrine cell populations monitor the water's other "ingredients."

The kidneys are unique in their location, as they are housed separately from the remaining abdominal organs. The abdomen houses organs that are wrapped in a lubricating sac called the peritoneum (ever heard of peritonitis? That's the name for what happens when this sac becomes infected). The kidneys, however, are located behind the peritoneum, wrapped in their own sac and tied to the lower ribs and upper lumbar spine.

The Latin word for kidney is *"rena."* Thus comes the name for the adrenal glands, a population of cells located on top of the kidneys. In the cellular realm, the adrenal glands produce adrenal hormones: epinephrine, cortisol, and others. In its mirror of the first chakra, *survival* involves the spacesuit's energy resources. The adrenal gland cell population deals with emergency or supplemental resources.

The adrenal glands do not function independently. They manufacture and secrete their hormones at a rate determined by the brain; in fact, they are regulated by a remarkable,primitive portion of the brain—and a relatively small one: the *hypothalamus*. The hypothalamus is no less than the interface between the nervous and endocrine organ/systems. It manufactures both hormones (for glands) and neurotransmitters (for neurons).

The brain, through the hypothalamus, oversees the *global energy needs* of the body, and adjusts the rate of adrenal hormones released at *any moment or any anticipated series of moments* as necessary. This is an amazing function, which has been studied in depth as part of the stress response, also known as the *"general adaptation syndrome."*

Just as the kidneys are unique in their location, the adrenal glands are unique in that they are derived from two primary germ layers. Remember the primary germ layers? Remember that the brain and nervous system derive from the ectoderm? Remember that the rest of the body derives from the middle layer, the mesoderm? Well, the inner portion of the adrenal glands, the *adrenal medulla*, grows from the ectoderm, while the outer portion, the *adrenal cortex*, grows from the mesoderm.

Now, let us imagine a stream of consciousness, shaded in red, pulsing through the blood stream from its source at the base of the spine. At the same time, imagine a stream of consciousness, shaded purple, pulsating down from an area in the middle of the forehead, through the blood, towards the heart, and from there to the kidneys in the mid-back.

Sit for a while and visualize. It's fun!

2. SWADHISTHANA: GONADS

The *swadhisthana chakra,* located in the region of the sacrum, embodies our sense of desire, creative output, and erotic attraction. Let us first consider desire, separate from erotic attraction. (We'll get back to that!) Desire, in the meaning understood in yoga philosophy, is called *"kama,"* and is understood as one of *four virtues.* Not to be confused with appetite, *kama* denotes our personal and aesthetic desires, the *forces* outside and within us that *attract* us to play a violin instead of a trumpet or watch a tragedy over a comedy, or study dance over basketball.

We saw that the organs associated with the first chakra purify the waters, the medium in which the spacesuit forms. The organs in the region of the second chakra are concerned with the formation of the spacesuit itself— the sequencing of its formation—as mirrored in the DNA molecule. The second chakra itself is concerned primarily with the problems of *reproduction* and *timing.*

The endocrine populations associated with the sacral chakra are called the *"gonads,"* a word meaning *"seeds"*—a good word, though only half true, for you will recall that, for us, reproduction manifests in the spacesuit as *sexual dimorphism.* Many diverse ways of uniting the two complementary pairs of different species have evolved. Fish deliver half seeds to the ocean bottom, while plants rely on wind or insects. Humans—for better, for worse—rely on our own signals and actions and on socially directed signals and actions—and hasn't that last part been fun over the last many millennia?

But then, it appears as though reproduction is meant to be difficult! Consider the odds of a *sperm* cell reaching an *ovum* (the male and female half-seeds, respectively). Sperm requires an alkaline environment to survive, whereas the mucous membranes lining the vaginal and fallopian walls are acidic—and therefore inhospitable to sperm. The entrance to the uterine cervix is narrow, and while the sperm swim upstream through the fallopian tubes, the tubes themselves are undergoing perpetual "sweeping" from "hairs" lining the tube and brushing in a downward movement. By the time an egg is reached by any sperm, the many millions of sperm cells that originally entered the vagina have been reduced to about fifty!

Sheesh! No wonder people feel tired when it's all over. Imagine how the cell people feel! We manifest, on the somatic realm in our spacesuits, the very work the half-seeds are doing in the cellular realm.

Erotic intimacy is one of the most extreme experiences of human pleasure. Contrast this with the experiences related to the first chakra, where our survival instincts can bring on our most enraged and defensive postures in response to extreme pain. If we consider the neuron cell people for a moment, the *senses* of both pain and pleasure are housed in the *limbic* regions of the brain. Their *responses,* in the extreme, are already programmed into the *hypothalamus.* These are called the rage and pleasure responses.

The rage and pleasure responses are orchestrated by the hypothalamus through two different types of neurons: *sympathetic* and *parasympathetic.* We met the sympathetic neurons that live in the thoracic region of the spine in the previous chapter. Recall also that the parasympathetic folk live in two places: the skull (at the base of the brain) and the sacrum (the triangular-shaped bone made of five fused parts located at the bottom of the spine).

Sympathetic neurons, when on full output, put in place a response we call the *fight or flight response.* (I'm partial to flight, myself!)

Parasympathetic neurons, on the other hand, manifest behavior that is calm, passive, and gentle. Purring kittens come to mind. Parasympathetic neurons are the population who respond to *arousal,* making us receptive, moist, and open to another spacesuit exchanging tremendous energy with ours. (Sympathetic neurons, however, are the cell population of *orgasm!*)

How poetically tricky. The sex act, carried through to orgasm, requires from us the delicate balance of remaining relaxed while the intensity of the fight or flight response grows and streams through our bodies.

The organs of second chakra are, like the organs of the first chakra, under the supervision and "timing" of not only the pituitary gland, but also the pineal glands in the skull. Timing in the spacesuit is absolutely crucial for the generating of half-seeds. Life begins in the waters, and living beings are a gift of the Earth to herself. Remember always that we're here for the needs of the Earth as much as we are for our individual and collective, or species-wide, needs.

From here, let us continue our visualization. Orange streams of desire float through our spacesuit, radiating out from the second chakra, attracting us to a color or sound, or a line of navel hair, or the curve of a cheek, or a smile or a voice. Desire is a sense easily accessed. As my kundalini yoga teacher says, "Contact that sweet second chakra, and share the energy with the rest of the chakras." How sweet!

So sit for a moment, and visualize orange streams radiating from the sacrum, through the bloodstream, where they are interwoven with the red streams emanating from the first chakra.

3. MANIPURA: PANCREAS

Let us begin the third chakra with a quick review. The organs of the first chakra purify the waters that are the medium for the maintenance of life in the cellular realm, of the spacesuit; while the second chakra generates the spacesuit itself.

The third chakra, *manipura,* is known to us as the solar plexus chakra. This region empowers and feeds the spacesuit, generating the fires that break down and absorb requisite nutrients from the atomic realm. In the subtle realm, it produces a stream of yellow light that circulates from the upper abdomen to everywhere else in the body. Its corresponding somatic endocrine organ, the pancreas, is under no influence other than the ecosystem of the blood itself. It is autonomous, independent of the great overseers, the hypothalamus and pituitary gland.

The pancreas is unusual as it is a dual gland, defined as both *exocrine* (secreting into a tube - like sweat) and *endocrine* (secreting directly into the blood.) As an exocrine gland, it makes enzymes and participates in the *digestion* and *absorption* of all types of food into the *blood and lymph.* As an endocrine gland, it is responsible for the absorption of a specific food into every *cell: glucose.*

Remember, we can tell if a molecule is important to the spacesuit when an entire population of cells is involved in its somatic interaction. Glucose has no less than five cellular populations involved in its maintenance, so it is obviously important.

It is in the abdomen that solid and liquid substances are processed and absorbed into the cells of the small intestine. From here, most of the food squeezes into the tiny veins, *ve-*

nules, which gather together to form larger veins, which then turn into a single, very large vein, the *hepatic portal vein.* If you've heard of the disease called *hepatitis,* then you may guess that this vein has something to do with the liver. (*Hepato* means "liver" in Greek.) The hepatic portal vein carries blood to the liver, and in this case, all the venous blood from every organ wrapped in the peritoneum, including the recently absorbed nutrients. (Fat is the one exception. Bypassing the venules, fat is absorbed into the *lymphatic vessels.* From there it goes on to the veins, emptying into the heart.)

I like to think of the liver as the *custom house* of the body because the liver *decides and selects,* among many things, what's food, what's poison, what passes through, what gets killed, filtered out, and shunted over to the gall bladder (where it will become part of the bile salts, and from there, part of tomorrow's fecal expression.) From the liver, the freshly processed solids and liquids travel to the heart—the right side of the heart, the side pumping blood to the lungs.

In the lungs, blood capillaries absorb the third food component, air, exchanging carbon dioxide for the oxygen in the air, so that by the time blood reaches the left side of the heart, all the solid, liquid, and air elements are freshly mixed like a fresh (albeit gooey) salad, ready for delivery in the blood to the cellular populations throughout the body.

Continuing our visualization, we now have tri-colored streams flowing through the body, the colors red, orange, and yellow. The yellow stream emanates from the third chakra. Sit for a moment and visualize those yellow streams radiating from the navel and lumbar regions, traveling through the bloodstream, and being interwoven with the red and orange streams emanating from the third chakra's companions, the earth-oriented first and second chakras.

4. ANAHATA: HEART AND THY-MUS GLAND

In the previous chapter, the movement of arterial blood down the arm in tandem with the movement of venous blood up the arm demonstrated parallel and complementary peripheral currents in the somatic realm. Now, if we continue to think of those blood vessels, and carry that same image all the way up the arm until we end (and begin!) at the heart, we can expand our comprehension of the electrified currents of blood to include the entire spacesuit.

How do we perceive the heart? Most of us are familiar with its function as a pump, having heard and felt its rhythmical tempo in ourselves and in others, such as our loved ones, our children, our clients, and our patients. Beating, however, is a sound. The heart beats. The heart has passive, fibrous "doors" called *"valves,"* which snap shut when the blood moves in one direction and open when the movement reverses. The heart sound we call a "beat" is the sound the fibrous doors make when they snap shut. So we know the heart beats, pumps blood, and makes a sound when its doors close.

The organs and systems within the anahata chakra mirror duality on multiple levels. In the early stages of heart development, there actually are two heart centers! One heart center, the one on the right, pumps blood to the developing lungs and returns blood to the second heart center, the one on the left. The second heart pumps blood to the embryo's tissue system wherein live all the cell people, and returns the blood back to the first heart. In its fully developed form, the two sides of the heart have joined, though they remain divided by a thick wall, a *septum.*

The heart is a unique neurological phenomenon in that it is the only muscle that does not require the nervous system to contract it. It has its own built-in self-starters (you've probably heard of pacemakers!) that self-electrify about seventy-five times a minute on average. The autonomic nervous system (sympathetic and parasympathetic cell people) can make adjustments to override, increasing or decreasing, the heart's basic rate of contraction.

The heart rate is directly dependent on the amount of oxygen needed at any moment in the spacesuit's activities. So if you're sitting in a chair, and then stand up, that represents a sudden need for oxygen delivery to the legs. This need is sensed by a cell population in the brain, which then signals the chest muscles and diaphragm to accelerate the breath rate, absorbing increased quantities of oxygen into the blood, while simultaneously signaling the heart to accelerate its pumping rate.

The heart sits on the diaphragm, smooshed in between the two lungs, with large blood vessels and the esophagus behind it, and the thymus gland cushioning it in front.

It is the *anahata chakra* we identify, when we say we have *love* for someone or something. Cupid and his arrows through someone's heart, love songs that speak of broken hearts, the imagery is abundant. The heart chakra is the place of compassion. It is the place of mercy. It is the place of recognition of our oneness with all beings. We learn this in our communities, our home, among our friends, lovers, and kin.

But as this world has duality, we find here in the fourth chakra, not only the cellular love- child hippies, but the cellular Navy Seals! Yes, sir! The white blood cells known as the T-lymphocytes cells are like the special forces of our spacesuit's defense system. And by defense systems, I refer to the systems in place to deal with toxic, microscopic entities—some living, some not—that enter the spacesuit, and how the cell people deal with them.

The thymus gland is the mirrored endocrine population, where primitive stem cells are transformed into T-lymphocytes or T-cells. Once developed, the T-cells form populations of direct killers. Unlike B-lymphocytes, which simply "shoot" biochemical antibodies from "cannons" throughout the spacesuit, the T-cells actually go to the site of the invader. Here we find a most unique method of defense: *Eat the enemy!* (It's a very efficient strategy by the way.)

So in the same region we find the loving energies that bring people together, coupled with the forces that specifically keep out "others." Among people, the forces of attraction and repulsions are colloquially referred to as "vibes."

Now we have four colored streams of light flowing through the body. The green stream of the fourth chakra is radiating and joining the energy of the other three. Sit for another moment and visualize this light radiating from the heart and thoracic regions, moving through the bloodstream, and being interwoven with the red, orange, and yellow streams.

5. VISHUDDHA: THYROID GLAND AND PARATHYROID GLANDS

The *vishuddha chakra*, located in the region of the throat, manifests the phenomenon of human speech, where one person's dialogue meets the collective consciousness. Language and the formation of vibrated air molecules that generate speech occur here. Air molecules carry streams of consciousness through space to be sensed.

Gods and goddesses speak to us, while we speak to each other.

The throat chakra is a place of differentiation. It is the anatomical location where solids and liquids are funneled to their appropriate tube, the *esophagus,* while air is directed into a separate tube leading to the lungs, the *trachea.* Blue streams of light radiate from here throughout the body, manifesting on the somatic realm as the thyroid gland and the parathyroid glands.

The thyroid gland contains one of the many cell populations that work with energy, again on a global level, and again with glucose. But where the first chakra revolved around supplemental, emergency energy resources and the third chakra was concerned with the absorption of glucose by cells, the vishuddha chakra deals with the efficiency or *rate* of energy manufacture. In the spacesuit, efficiency expresses itself in the number of *worker enzymes* present in each cell at any time. The more enzymes present, the more efficient is the manufacture (metabolism) of energy by cell populations.

In physiology, this rate is described as the spacesuit's basal metabolic rate (BMR). The hormone called *thyroid hormone* is responsible for regulating this rate. As the metabolism is a global matter, the brain monitors the entirety of this process. When the global energy output decreases, so does the spacesuit's BMR, at which point the brain will signal the pituitary gland to signal the thyroid gland to put out less thyroid hormone.

Phew!

The thyroid gland has two other populations of cells living on either side of it, the *parathyroid glands. Para* means "to the side." The parathyroid glands deal with a single element from the atomic realm: calcium. We've already gotten a sense of how important glucose is to the body, recognizing five endocrine populations devoted to its balance. Let's look at calcium and get a sense of even more complexity, and its special relationship with sunshine. (Or, if you've had enough, skip to the next section!)

The elements of the atomic realm have generated a complex interactive strategy among the cellular populations for the maintenance of calcium. The very presence of calcium in the blood is dependent on a transformation sequence that begins with sunlight turning a molecule in the skin into a second molecule. (This is the closest we come to being plants!) This second molecule travels into the blood where it is changed into a third molecule by the liver, which is transformed again into a fourth molecule by the lungs, which finally travels to the small intestine as vitamin D. Vitamin D as a nutrient is necessary in order for the calcium you eat to become absorbed into the blood through the small intestine. That's how cells cooperate!

Calcium is used in many important processes in our space-suit. It is necessary for neurons to transmit signals, for muscles to contract, and for blood vessels to heal. It is the stuff of bones, the rock-like crystals that give bones the strength necessary for the muscles to pull against. And the calcium crystals found at the base of the inner-ear hairs amplify the magical patterns vibration that flow through the waters of the inner ear, generating the sensation that we call "sound."

Remember when the monster in the movie *The Bride of Frankenstein* hears music coming from his blind neighbor's violin? He grasps at the air, trying to "catch" the sounds as they move inside him, penetrating his very essence—invisible, intangible, and delightful. This was a moment of incredible insight from film monster history. Sometimes science fiction isn't so fictitious, right?

Calcium ions circulate throughout the bloodstream and are found in quantities within a specific range. This range is monitored by the parathyroid glands in the region of the throat chakra. The parathyroid populations somehow "sense" the *amount* of calcium floating around them. The amount must be kept strictly within range, for extremes on either side (too much or too little) render the cell dysfunctional. The glands are interactive with the bones of the spacesuit. Bones contain our calcium storage, and when blood levels are lowered or raised, the bones respond.

Two important cells work on bone construction. Both types have the prefix *"osteo"* because *osteo* means "bone." *Osteoblasts* build up and concentrate bone material, making them thicker and stronger, and thereby store excess calcium. *Osteoclasts* break down bone, "chewing up" small pieces, and "spitting" them into the blood, thereby raising the amount of circulating calcium. The range of calcium in the blood is maintained by osteoclasts chewing faster or slower; and the rate of chewing is controlled by the hormones sent out by the parathyroid glands.

This is already a very complicated interaction for a single element, and yet there is one more feature to add. As we age, our pineal gland accumulates calcium. It is my guess that, since calcium is the amplifying crystal for sound, it also serves as an amplifying crystal for the soul's ability to tune-in to the subtle realms outside our spacesuit, preparing us for the Great Transition when the soul leaves the spacesuit for good. But that's only my own personal theory!

So now we can add a fifth stream to our rainbow of flowing streams of consciousness: a sky-blue shade interwoven with the remaining four.

How beautiful! Sit for a moment and see this shade emanating from our throat to the entirety of the spacesuit.

6. AJNA: PITUITARY GLAND

The Gospel of Matthew says, "The light of the body is the eye, and if thine eye be single, thy whole body shall be filled with light." This is expressed in other ways, such as in the images of lifting thine eyes up to heaven or of a dove descending from heaven. Mystics throughout time have described a light embedded somewhere in our forehead, and this is the *ajna chakra*, which is the seat of the willful intention in our spacesuit. In the subtle realm, it is shaded a deep, indigo blue.

This energy center manifests on the somatic realm as the pituitary gland, which physiology terms the *"master gland."* Found in an ancient portion of the brain, the pituitary gland produces nine different hormones, all under the control of the hypothalamus. Four of the nine hormones deal with reproductive timing, while three deal with metabolism. Of the remaining two hormones, one directs the kidneys in water retention, while the second affects the skin cells responsive to sunlight.

The pituitary gland is physically connected to the hypothalamus, which is the source overseeing every autonomic organ in the spacesuit. When we speak of global somatic issues, we are somehow talking about the hypothalamus. Located in the region of the *ajna chakra*, the hypothalamus orchestrates the visceral responses of rage, passivity, hunger, thirst, and satiety.

In addition to visceral responses, the *ajna chakra* is also the center of our willful activity. On the somatic realm, we find willfulness mirrored in the regions of the brain associated with stored memory, in an area physiologists refer to as the *"pre-mo-*

tor cortex." This regulates habitual movements practiced so much that they appear to be automatic. Such movements are learned, repeated over time, stored as "memory" in the brain, and accessible to us by volition.

Consider for a moment your left arm, hanging relaxed at your side. Imagine your arm moving forward, elbow straight, fingers gently extended. Although you perceive no actual movement, the brain is already setting up a pattern of muscle contraction, anticipating and preparing a contraction sequence based on your thought alone! This is referred to as a subliminal stimulation of the muscles—there is enough electricity to get them started energetically, but not enough for a full contraction. The brain is anticipating your next move.

After you have sat with the imagined motion for a while, actualize it by moving the arm in front of you. What's the difference? As far as the brain is concerned, very little. As far as the muscles and bones, a lot has changed! The difference is that little, invisible piece we call will!

Fred Alan Wolfe has written a beautiful little book called *Mind into Matter,* which plays with this image through the perspective of a quantum physicist: modern mysticism. If you are looking for more of details along these lines, check him out! He's awesome, and very funny!

As we have seen, the *ajna chakra* is the interface between autonomic and voluntary activities, between the endocrine and nervous organ/systems, between witness and actor. Yet, returning to St. Matthew, the sixth chakra is also the literal *focal point* for access by the individual spacesuit person to the greater realm of Spirit through the phenomenon of the third eye. The world's mystical testimony affirms the existence of the "light" within, depicted as a luminous, single "eye" bordered with an outer, narrow orange/yellow sphere, which surrounds a wider, deep blue sphere surrounding a bright, star-like center—the doorway to the infinite.

The doorway is perceived when the eyes are converged at a point projected above, between, and forward from the eyebrows: the third-eye position. It is an amazing light. As one focuses in an ever more concentrated manner, the power of that center begins to vibrate the chakra centers one by one, presenting the inner, astral body sounds to our inner hearing. Although language and symbols differ throughout time and tradition, the images are mutually resonating.

I once attended the funeral of a great aunt at a Greek Orthodox church in Hoboken, New Jersey with a yogi companion. Being a time for contemplation, I decided to meditate. The rituals and chants were familiar, and provided a comforting background. I began with my eyelids half-closed. As I gazed up and forward into third-eye position, in the ceiling directly in line with my gaze I saw a visual aid. There in the rounded dome of the church was a stained-glass rendering of a candle with a white flame and holder, surrounded by a blue heaven, all wrapped in an orange-yellow halo!

Sound familiar? Didn't I just describe the third eye with those shades of white, blue and orange? You see, the ancients knew about this third eye business. Ancient traditions continued to depict the third eye in sacred art and architecture. Yet many of the ancient symbols, though represented, lost their meanings over time, and were forgotten—for awhile anyway. Many of us today are remembering.

My companion and I both noticed the stained-glass visual aid at the same time, and smiled at each other in conspiratorial recognition of our ancient oneness.

Let's add a sixth color to add to our streams of consciousness. The deep, indigo blue is not interwoven with the remaining five colors, but rather surrounds them. Sit for a moment and see this shade emanating from your throat to the entirety of your spacesuit.

7. SAHASRARA: PINEAL GLAND

The *sahasrara chakra* is our connection to the Divine. Divine, deva, devotion, devotee. All these words speak of *forces* within and without that drive us toward that which we speak of as higher planes of consciousness and existence. The word *"sahasrara"* translates as "thousand-petalled lotus," which is a description of the cosmic streams of energy perceived by the mystics to be radiating from this chakra.

Physical light directly affects the spacesuit in three identifiable populations of cells: those that live in the retinas of the physical eyes, those that darken the skin, and those that live in the pineal gland, the organ which mirrors the seventh chakra. The pineal gland secretes the hormone *melatonin* in response to the subtle density of sunlight.

The pineal gland was, at one time, an actual third eye, in some ancient reptilian life form. In our spacesuit, pineal stimulation comes from the binocular reception of sunlight on the retinas of the two physical eyes—or rather from the absence of sunlight. For it is in the evening that the secretions occur. Melatonin affects the rate at which the ovaries and spermaries develop half-seeds. In mammals other than humans, the rate is connected to timing so that when birthing takes place, it does so in the spring! Estrus cycles in animals are timed in this manner, what we refer to as a female animal being "in heat."

Not true for humans, however, as the timing of birth isn't limited to environmental constraints. This is what the social scientists have named the "permanent sexual receptivity of the human female." (Wishful thinking, if you ask me!)

The sahasrara chakra is the place of contact with the larger self, the place of intuition and mystical awareness. The word "mystical" comes from root words meaning *"with eyes closed."* Isn't that cool? It is no coincidence that the "light of the body" is seen with the eyes closed. The withdrawing of the physical senses is necessary in order to perceive the subtle dimensions. In the Yoga Sutras of Patanjali, he calls such withdrawal *"pratayahara."*

One more relevant point about the pineal gland needs to be mentioned before we leave this chapter. It has been recently discovered that the pineal gland manufactures the hallucinogenic molecule *dimethyl triptamine.* This is the same agent found in peyote cactus, psyllosybin mushrooms, and on a vine that grows in the Amazon rain forest, which is smoked for the purpose of mystical experience by the natives there, who call it *"ayuhuasca."* It has been proposed that this molecule is responsible for the ecstatic experiences reported by mystics and shamans alike, and that prolonged meditation stimulates its release.

The sahasrara chakra is our direct connection to the ultimate source of subtle energy: God, Allah, the One, Brahman. The goal of meditation involves the opening of this center, joining with it, and thereby *melding* with the One—or something like that. The yogis call this melding *"samadhi,"* the breathless state. We'll speak more about this in our next and final chapter.

Our final stream of consciousness is upon us. Visualize a deep, purple stream flowing from the sahasrara chakra, at the crown of your skull, the soft spot of a newborn. It surrounds and penetrates the other six streams, and the combined sound emanating from the seven centers is given a name: Om! Aum! Amen! Sit for a moment, and see this shade emanating from our skull to the entirety of the spacesuit, joining and harmonizing with its sister and brother streams.

You are that!

Chapter 7

The Soul of Community

The Entirety of Humanity as an Organism

"Religion brought me to politics, and those who think religion and politics have nothing to do with each other know neither religion nor politics."
—Mahatma Gandhi

S it for a moment and imagine, once again, your spacesuit filled with tiny cell people who are working together to keep you in a continuous state of being. A colossal organization of energy, consciousness, and love is flowing through you, allowing you to be you. Feel the energy. Feel the motions within: your breath, your heart, and even your stomach rumbling. Your senses, your thoughts, and the emotions that arise from your thoughts, are all part of a living, breathing, and self-maintaining miracle: You! Your body! Your spacesuit!

Enjoy it for a few minutes.

Om! Shanti!

A LITTLE EARTH SCIENCE

The nature of the manifest universe presents itself as imitation, multiplication, and condensation in a cooperative dance among complementary and opposing forces. It is in this context that the story and history of life on Earth takes place. The ancestors for *true cells* are found fossilized in rock from far back in time, over two and a half billion years ago. These first beings were anaerobic, breathing in an atmosphere rich in carbon dioxide, and breathing out oxygen. Though lacking a nucleus, they possessed the ability to transform sunlight into carbohydrate. As noted before, today we know these organisms as blue-green algae.

Now consider: It took these *proto-cells* around two billion of years to breathe out enough oxygen to make possible the existence of an oxygen-rich atmosphere, enough to make possible the eukaryotes, or true cells, of which our bodies are composed. The period when eukaryotes first appear is called the Paleozoic Era, which began about 550 million years ago.

The salient feature of life on the Earth is the cooperative condensation of matter and energy in a world of complementary and opposed energies, and its consequence: increasing densities. Life adapts to geologic changes on Earth, gradually generating more complicated communication systems. We have seen how our spacesuits house a sensory system that depends on five densities available in our external and internal environment.

To view our spacesuit's existence as dependent on the cooperative and synchronized activities of trillions of little cell people is frightening enough, but reconsider this: We sit and move on a living planet that is held in place by some unknown force called "gravity," pulling at us from within a core we know very little about, and, further, we are captured in an orbit around a *very* hot ball of energy. Whatever forces may hold our planet and the Sun together and keep us pulled just close enough, but not too far away for life to exist, obviously there is a delicate *balance* holding all this explosive energy and matter together.

Where does this leave us, as a species of individuals? It leaves us with each other: in community! The principle of cooperation in our universe has driven us to greater cooperation between members of our species. Although history offers much evidence to the contrary, cooperation is our species-wide gift, and our multiple world cultures are developing into a planetary consciousness. We are faced with issues, problems, and solutions that can only be resolved on a global scale, among people who perceive themselves as a world community. We hear and speak much about competition, globalization, and the organization of the world on commercial principles, yet we also possess a sense of planetary consciousness. To use the recent saying: "Think Global, Act Local."

We recognize that somehow it is in collective action that the problems of our times will be resolved. This drive towards cooperation and community is consistent with the way the universe operates, and it is the only way our species has survived through its very long history.

Let us return for a moment to the atomic realm, electrically balanced, self-contained entities with equal numbers of light particles call electrons, protons, and neutrons. Arranged like a planetary solar system on Ritalin, they contain a fixed "solar" center, the nucleus, and orbiting "planets," the electrons. And what do they do all day? Attract and repulse each other in the formation of energy bonds.

Now consider the somatic realm. A person is a self-contained entity and, like an atom, needs people in order to bond, to form connections that complete that person, that define and generate a context within the life of that person. A person has friends, lovers, families, coworkers, neighbors, and enemies whom it is attracted to, and repulsed by in varying degrees.

The human need for community is the obvious conclusion that people who work together can accomplish something, and even more. For working together is, in the final analysis, the only way we've ever accomplished anything significant. It's what we have as a species-wide survival tool. It is why anthropology defines us as *social beings*.

The soul of community is inherent in the very nature of our species, as a part of the grand-scale cooperation of the complementary forces in the matrix of the universe. The phenomenon of cooperation, of unity of opposites, is the structural basis of our universe, and it is expressed in each and every one of its planes of magnification or realms of existence.

The soul of community, the social practice of cooperation, is inherent in the cell, which is a microscopic spacesuit consisting of trillions of molecules made of spliced and unspliced atoms, themselves little lightrons of what? *Prana?* Tiny particles of conscious love? The manifest universe gets as small as it is huge.

The soul of community is inherent in our spacesuit, where there are trillions of cell people cohabiting, themselves differentiated into specific working groups to keep this body alive within, while we do what we do: move, work with our hands, speak, breathe, make love, read, think, exercise, pray, and even, yes, kill. We are here to dance with each other, with the Earth, and with Spirit.

RELIGIOUS PRACTICE

It is impossible to speak of these things without discussing the "R" word, *religion*. Paramahansa Yogananda's definition of religion is a great starting point, for he equates religion with the word *"yoga."*

The word "religion" comes from the Latin roots *"re"* and *"ligare."* Meaning, "to tie, bind again, reconnect." And so, in this view, a religious practice is any action that reunites our sense of being an individual within a larger truth, a larger whole, a larger self, a practice that awakens our compassion and humanity.

The word "yoga" comes from the Sanskrit root *"yuj,"* which means something similar: "to join, unite, yoke." Religion is therefore the Latin equivalent to yoga, that which reconnects the personal *self* with the larger *Self*, aka Spirit.

In this context then, let us reconsider the question: What qualifies as a religious practice? What actions remind us of our larger Self? The answer: Potentially every action of our lives. Religious practices are soul exercises.

The ancients understood that human activity is sacred and reveled in community practices, including prayers, chants, and rituals for every occasion. Remnants and hints of ancient sacredness still remain with us in modern times; these are found in all areas of our personal lives and social traditions. They may not be remembered as sacred practices, and their spiritual amplification may be ignored or over-looked, yet our deep *whispering* spaces are nurtured by these sacred traditions.

Let us explore some of the community religious practices.

SPORTS

We think of visual sports as entertainment, where honoring the victors with fame and fortune is the expectation. Yet, the ancients who organized the Olympics or the Aztecs who played sacred games recognized sports as activity honoring and dedicated to the Pantheon of Gods and Goddesses. This recognition brought the geographically diverse community together in their mythical assumptions and spiritual practice.

Today people who attend and follow sporting events still experience the sense of a larger community, a larger sense of Self. In our hearts, somewhere, though we don't consider the gods, we nevertheless know that luck has a lot to do with winning. Through this community religious practice we feel an increased sense of brotherhood and sisterhood with fellow fans, a symptom of any religious activity (especially when our team wins).

THEATER

Ancient theater represented a culmination of traditions dating back to the Neolithic Era. When power stories like *Gilgamesh, Beowulf, The Iliad,* and *The Mahabharata* were told by itinerant bards, people danced in circles, lit fires, burned incense, and consumed substances in honor and remembrance of the immortal forces of the universe. Classical theater is an evolution of these ancient practices, designed to accommodate larger, more localized populations. In the place of traveling bards visiting dispersed communities, the audiences gathered at theatrical centers. Script composition incorporated the elements of the power stories and rituals, while synthesizing the elements of dance, song, and story. The consciousness of the audience was elevated, experiencing greater awareness and appreciation for life and its blessings. Theatric festivals lasted many days, and the presentations, alternating Tragedy with Comedy, always ended with a Comedy!

Today, again viewed as entertainment, something to do on a Friday night, we nevertheless come out of a good movie, like *Gandhi*, with a shared sense of spiritual elevation. Greater wisdom has been implanted, as well a greater desire for peace. The effect is, again, due to the religious nature of theater.

RITUAL

Group prayer, meditation, and ritual are our most familiar forms of community religious practice. Ritual in the West contains many of the elements of ancient theater: tones, anti-tones, chorus, protagonist, death, and rebirth. Ritual combines the profound elements of tragedy and comedy with an equally profound reverence.

In the right mindset, people leave a ritual with a feeling of greater connection to self, family, people, and Spiritod. The intent of community religious gatherings, organized or not, is to instill this same feeling of uplifting and inspiration.

DANCE OF THE FAMILY

My family of origin is Greek, having arrived here in the early 1900s. I grew up in a familial ghetto of Greeks in an old world-style extended immigrant family with eight siblings and two parents who braved the change. During my early youth, the first generation (my parents and their siblings and cousins) spent most of their available social time with each other and their children, we of the second generation. It was a *colorful* period with over twenty exotic and deliciously gustatory households to visit, play in, and generally feel safe, in a tribal sense.

In this community, the sense of family obligation (there's that root again: *ligare*) was strong. Every holiday and social gathering took place at some sponsoring relatives' home. Their hospitality extended to friends of family members, and it was not unusual to attend gatherings of over one hundred people. The women and men labored all day and evening with food preparation. (Men were rarely involved with clean-up. They could be found gambling and arguing over cards!) By the time I was in my early twenties, that had all disappeared and the modernization of my family was complete. The breakup of the extended family and its byproduct, the nuclear family, is an historical phenomenon unprecedented in our specie's history. (The movie *Avalon* deals with this theme in a most lovely manner.)

Yet in spite of the issues resulting from the confinement and alienation of the nuclear family, as it did in my experience, many of us come out with a sense of belonging, of connection, of home. (By the way, it seems to me no coincidence that the root sound *"Om"* is at the center of the word "home"!) This sense of our larger Self, this sense of connection, is, again, one that I would consider religious. We intuitively know something about our common unity.

Yogananda reminds us that the lessons provided in our family relations are the prototype for our adult social practice;

that here in our families, we learn about love, compassion, authority, forgiveness, tyranny, and cooperation. We learn about brotherhood from our brothers and sisterhood from our sisters.

As a young adult I had lived in what was known as a "commune" in the 1970s, but what the hippies now would call an "intentional community." We were intent on redefining the family, living with people we called our "brothers and sisters," and developing a theory and practice for cooperative living, personal growth, and childcare. This new form of family exceeded my expectations for personal and spiritual growth, and provided all of us (eventually six adults and four kids) with a solid foundation, which we took to new places after living together for fifteen years.

THE DANCE OF CHILDREARING

The primary function of the family is the raising of the next generation. If you've been blessed by the receiving of an infant in your life, and seeing him or her through to adulthood, then there's little I need to say. Childcare is a religious experience. We just don't call it that.

My son, Andreas (Andy) is to date my greatest teacher. He teaches me while I witness and nurture his life processes: his physical development, his joyful youth, his increasingly nihilistic adolescence (Oy!), and his burgeoning young adult phases. As of this writing, he is twenty-four and raising a baby girl. Andy teaches me as I witness myself interact with him: my vocal tones, my conscious actions, my reactions, my wisdom, my foolishness, my cruelties, and my sense of service to him.

THE DANCE OF EROTIC LOVE

The mythologies of our culture present lovemaking as the

hallmark of success and happily ever after, while the pulpits and censors simultaneously dismiss and denounce it as the bed of evil. We are a very, very confused nation on the subject. Yet our practice and experience whispers to us of sexuality's sacredness. The concentrating of energies into the second chakra explodes and fills all the others, temporarily giving us a physiological rush. The yogis call this *"shaktipat."* We, of course, call it an "orgasm."

The experiments and writings of Wilhelm Reich revealed the energetic nature of the orgasmic experience on the cellular, psychological, somatic and even political levels. Being a strict Freudian, and therefore assuming all psychophysical problems stem from sexual repression, Reich called sexual energy *"orgone."* Yet the more one studies his work, the parallels of orgone energy to *prana* and *chi* are astounding.

The blending of two (or more) loving bodies in a synergistically charged experience is the spark that invites communion with another's soul—in friendship, in trust, and in love. In addition and under the right circumstances, it also invites new souls from the subtle realms that need a spacesuit to enter into our planet of delights: conception. As we merge with the spacesuits of others, we expand ourselves in a field of energy, temporarily glimpsing the possibilities of melding with Spirit. For many mortals, even those of a non-mystical bent, a sense of the infinite is hinted at through the intimate union with a loved one - truly a religious experience.

It's why we scream, "O God!"

GOVERNMENT

Surprised? Yes, even the government contains elements and practices traceable to our sacred past. The protocols of greetings, openings, and in-swearings of official events and persons attest to the anachronistic and nevertheless ecclesiastic origins of our government and judicial procedures. "In God We Trust" is printed on our money, though the constitutionality of this has been a question since the Civil War, when it was first initiated. The very notion of democracy, the simultaneous dream of Utopia and the recollected Garden of Eden, testifies to an innate appreciation of our social and species-wide possibilities.

LABOR/WORK

Human artistry and invention was recognized as a sacred gift and practice in ancient times. Social activities related to agriculture (preparing the earth, planting seed, maintenance of the garden, and harvesting) were initiated and maintained with prayers, rituals, sacrifices, and celebrations. Gods and goddesses were thanked for their gifts and honored in recognition of the community's complete vulnerability to the planetary forces and elements.

Craftsmen, too, were perceived as magical. As we gaze into the eyes of children while they watch an artisan build a house, fix a truck, or turn a potter's wheel, we remember the sense of marvel that too often gets lost in our modern state of commercial bedazzlement. Robert Graves, the great English translator of the ancient Greek myths, recounts the story of the one-eyed monster, the Cyclops. In Homer's *Odyssey*, the "one eye" in the center of Polyphemus' forehead represents, among other things, the circular tattoos worn by smiths and other ancient metalworkers, also in the middle of the forehead.

Priestly, scholarly, and healing professionals were regarded as possessing some quality of inspiration, as they are to this day.

All professional activities back then took place within cultures that recognized the gifts of talent as being divinely inspired. Today, by contrast, there is little sense of reverence in the modern workplace. Yet, we also feel a sense of pride at having produced our creations, be it a hamburger, a glass bottle off an assembly line, a painting, or a soothed patient. We recognize the *magic* of human activity in every aspect of our collective endeavors, for human activity is in fact sacred, and that sacredness is carried over to the object of our activity.

When a person performs an activity, he or she performs it first in the mind, and then the spacesuit translates the intent into an action. Be our action the manipulation of a piece of clay, whittling a piece of wood with a knife into a shape, or baking a loaf of bread, we recognize that raw materials have been transformed into something that contains *magic*. Of course, we don't call it *magic*. We call it *"value."*

The most famous proponent of the labor theory of value was Karl Marx, who took his cues from David Ricardo and ultimately, from Adam Smith. Utopians of the nineteenth century dreamed a great and worldwide social vision, and associated the words "socialism" and "communism" with that vision. The oriental despotism that called itself Communism in the twentieth century is not to be confused with the Utopian vision. Recall that even *democracies* in the United States and elsewhere were also based originally on some form of slavery or indentured servant system, combined with an agenda for land aggrandizement that did not exclude the systematic genocide of the people here! Yet, some dream is still kicking inside us.

The propensity for cooperation with each other, combined with our appreciation for objects created by human hands, qualify work as a religious practice.

We are sacred beings, and everything we do has the potential for sacredness. It's up to each of us to realize this simple truth.

"Love, Work and Democracy are the Wellsprings of Life.
They should also Govern It."
—Wilhelm Reich

START ANYWHERE,
END UP
EVERYWHERE!
—MICHAEL
ROSEN-PYROS

Chapter 8

In Closing

"Dharma is the thread that integrates all the lives we experience."
—Venkatakrishna Sastry, lecture on
"Principles of Hinduism"

As he was surrendering to Isaac Stevens, Governor of Washington Territory in 1855, Chief Seattle, the leader of the Suquamish People of the Northwest Coast, spoke these words: "The Earth does not belong to us, we belong to the Earth." The words are now emblazoned on bumper stickers throughout the United States, and are an appeal to what is obvious to many of us. Although we fear the modern process that goes by the name of globalization, we nevertheless also sense increased awareness and interest in planetary consciousness. The Earth and nature have in fact been ravaged, plundered, bitten, and polluted, and it's our job to fix it.

In the 1960s, environmentalist and futurist James Lovelock introduced the Gaia hypothesis: the idea that the Earth is a single, self-regulating system. He compared it to a cell. He chose to address the Earth in the form known to the ancient Greeks, *Gaia*. Once again, the Earth started to be viewed as a living entity and the concepts of *ecology* and *bioregionalism* became public discussions.

The English language both hides and verifies the Gaia hypothesis. In Latin, *mater* translates as "mother." Surprisingly, *mater* is also the root of the word "material." What we perceive and denote as material reality and, in fact, all material wealth, comes from Gaia, our Mother Earth, and our interactions with her.

Our task is nothing less than turning swords into plowshares, a wish that has occupied our species since the invention of war. This writer believes wholeheartedly that people have the ability to realize this. It is part of our very nature. When we find ourselves seeing and loving the Earth as a living being, generating and sustaining all life, then loving her is automatic. The clarity derived from that love makes it so much easier for each of us to do the right thing.

Let's investigate this concept a little bit more.

DHARMA: RIGHT ACTION

In Hindu philosophy, the idea of "doing the right thing" is given a name: *dharma*. *Dharma* is the sustainer of the universe, the cosmic container. In a personal sense, *dharma* describes an individual's "way," the sum total of his or her actions, as seen over a lifetime or even in the moment. Our individual lives are a microcosm of the dharma of the Universe. Dharma refers to the path we walk in life, to our goals and aspirations. This concept is similar to what the Chinese philosopher Lao Tzu describes in his portrayal of Tao, or balanced nature, in the *Tao Te Ching.*

In light of this, the actions we take and the choices we make based on our assumptions, and the testing of those assumptions through action, imply an inner sense of *dharma*, both on a universal and personal level. Native American tradition takes this even further, as it considers the effect of our actions on the next seven generations. We are viewed merely as caretakers.

This beautiful and simple Native American sentiment leads me to imagine how wonderful this planet Earth would be if we created policies and institutions that addressed the needs of our children for the next seven generations. I imagine children would not only feel welcomed by their parents, but by the entire world community if we did.

Actions that are in accordance with *dharma* are not limited to the philosophy of Hinduism. They are universal and consistent with common sense. They resonate with our hearts and therefore are found throughout the world's catalogue of human scriptures and stories. They are known as *yamas* and *niyamas* in yoga philosophy. They are summarized in the Golden Rule, familiar to most of us, and include abstaining from killing, lying, stealing, raping, and overconsumption, and instead manifesting kindness, gentleness, harmlessness, inquisitiveness, and showing as much patience to your brothers and sisters as you would to yourself.

The great rabbi Jesus of Nazareth promised that the "peacemakers will be called blessed." Justice, mercy, and peace on Earth with good will toward men, women, and the next seven generations are implied in these statements.

We *can* do all this. It's just a question of how. We have created air flight and skyscrapers. We can't create a garden? Of course we can!

LOVE THE EARTH
AND HER CREATURES.
LOVE EACH OTHER.
AND DON'T FORGET TO
LOVE YOURSELF!
NAMASTE.

Afterword: Voices from the Realms

The body's (Somatic) perspective. "I am you. You are me. You see me in a mirror. I am alive. I need social, physical, nutritional, economic, familial, and spiritual replenishment to accommodate my insatiable need to have food, shelter, clothing, meaningful work, love, family, friendships, and, of course, sex." Like my mother says, "I love my little life!" *Amin.*

A cell's perspective. "Ha! The truth is, you are nothing! I am the guy, *numero uno!* I know you think it's all about you, but you are my slave . . . a slave to my insatiable need to have metabolisms of many kinds. Metabolic processes keep me (and all my ninety-plus trillion brother and sister cell-people) alive. By the way, metabolic processes keep you alive! I matter, but you really don't exist. You are a figment of our collective cellular imagination. I hope you're enjoying the show." *Allah akbar!*

An atom's perspective. "Okay, let me let you in on a little secret. That cell guy! I love watching and listening to him go on and on about himself! He thinks it's all about him, but of course he is nothing more than the cooperative love between my brother and sister atoms, and our insatiable need to manifest attractions, repulsions, and magnetic bonding with each other." *Shalom!*

The Earth's perspective. "You are me! My body is perfused

and covered with life, joy, consciousness, and love, while your body is an inverted mirror of myself, and has life enclosed within it. I love you, and my plant children need you to expire: to breathe out regularly and feed them with fresh carbon dioxide, while you fertilize my soil with your processed droppings, drippings, and other scats. My love is expressed everywhere you perceive, and is manifested in the relations between you and me and between you and your brother and sister life forms. Remember me always." *Aho!*

A soul's perspective. "In the end, yes, my brother, my sister, I'm the one who energizes, attracts, and generates the form you call your body, assembling these atoms, cells, and organ/systems to house me . . . that is, you, the you that remains after the body has had enough. I am beyond time, beyond space, an electric, phenomenal being with unlimited joy in my immersion with the infinite—and it's all yours, for the asking." *Namaste!*

Acknowledgments

Many people, over much time, have added to the thoughts leading to *Life in a Spacesuit*, many who know and love me, except for Tom Leimert. When he offered to read my almost last draft, I was elated. We had just met over the phone, discussing topics taught in anatomy for yoga teachers, and the subject of the book came up. Tom is a retired oncologist in Oregon who now teaches yoga, grows vegetables, and behaves like a Greek-American papou to his kids. So when he offered to read my next draft, and expressed kudos with each installment, I was even more encouraged to finish.

Joni Masse read and commented on more experiments and copy than I can count, and is still interested in the project! A special thanks to you, lady.

Paramahansa Yogananda, Fred Alan Wolf and all of the great teachers of science and mysticism who attempt to bring it all together, they are my inspirations.

The elders of the Pyros family had a mystical and left-radical slant to their views of the world. They started me questioning, well, everything, and so great thanks to you all for teaching me to reverently question authority as a young man.

My sister, Christine Saris and Dana Padgett, both massage therapists, asked if they could help me in my project as illustrators. The lovely drawings contained within this book are just a sample of what they offered me. (I hope the next edition can reproduce them in color.)

My cousin (and mentor), Dean Tsonas, read just one chapter and told me not to be so glib! Cost me seventy pages. (Lucky for the reader.)

Professor Venkatakrishna Sastry of Hindu University of America in Orlando, FL, who gave me permission to use his exquisite quote from his lecture on dharma.

Gus Yoo, the interior and exterior designer of this project, sent me his first proofs. and I was shocked when I realized how pretty this project could be.

Stephanie Gunning, who line edited the project and otherwise directs every step I take from herein, had grokked my concept of the Universe of Many Dimensions contained within us, and turned my apoplectic style into beautiful prose.

I thank you all.

Recommended Reading

ANATOMY AND PHYSIOLOGY

Arthur Guyton, *Basic Neuroscience*, second edition.
Philadelphia, PA: W.B. Saunders Co., 1991.

Gerard J. Tortora, *Principles of Anatomy and Physiology*,
thirteenth edition. Hoboken, N.J.: John Wiley and Sons,
2012.

Lewis Thomas, *The Lives of a Cell: Notes of a Biology* Watcher.
New York: Viking Press, 1974.

EARTH AWARENESS AND COMMUNITY

Communities Magazine, which is published by the Fellowship for
Intentional Community, has been writing about, and
organizing communities around the world since the
1970s. Their website is a treasure chest of information on
community in both theory and practice: FIC.ic.org

James Lovelock, *Gaia: A New Look at Life on Earth*, third
edition. London, U.K.: Oxford University Press, 2000.

Raymond Bridge, *The Geology of Boulder County.* Denver,
CO.: Geological Survey Society, 2004.

David C. Roberts, *A Field Guide to Geology.* New York:
Houghton Mifflin, 1996.

QUANTUM PHYSICS AND QABALA

Fred Alan Wolf, *Mind Into Matter*. Needham, MA: Moment
Point Press, 2000.

Matter into Feeling. Needham: Moment Point Press, 2002.

Carlo Suares, *Cipher of Genesis.* Boston: Shambhala
  Publications, 1970.

YOGA AND MYSTICISM
Swami Sri Yukteswar, *The Holy Science.* Los Angeles, CA.:
  Self-realization Fellowship, 1949.
Paramahansa Yogananda, *Autobiography of a Yogi,* Los Angeles,
  CA.: Self-realization Fellowship Press, 1971.
Paramahansa Yogananda, *The Science of Religion*, Los Angeles,
  CA.: Self-realization Fellowship Press, 1953.
Sri Swami Satchitananda, *Yoga Sutras of Patanjali.*
  Buckingham, VA: Integral Yoga Publications, 1990.

MYTHOLOGY
Robert Graves, *The Greek Myths.* London, U.K: Penguin
  Books, 1955.
William Buck, *The Mahabharata.* Los Angeles, CA.:
  University of California Press, 2000.

BODY-ENERGY
Wilhelm Reich, *The Bioelectric Investigation of Sexuality and
  Anxiety.* New York: Farrar, Straus, and Giroux, 1982.
Niclaire Mann and Eleanor McKenzie, *Thai Bodywork.*
  London: Octopus Publishing Group, 2002.
Vasant Lad, Ayurveda: *The Science of Self-Healing.* Wilmot:
  Lotus Press, 1984.

About the Author

MICHAEL ROSEN-PYROS, B.A., D.C.

"For me, the Human Sciences are a sacred study, and teaching is an opportunity to share my 'homework' with fellow colleagues, students and patients." (MR-P) Michael began teaching Kinesiology, Yoga and Tai Chi in 1984, offering classes to the general public in his chiropractic office. He is the former owner/director of the Sarasota School of Massage Therapy, where he taught subjects in the Human Sciences for 20 years. He has more recently provided classes for Yoga Teacher Programs around the Tampa Bay area. Michael received his B.A. Liberal Arts in 1975 at SUNY, Old Westbury. He attended the New York Chiropractic College, receiving his D.C. degree in 1983. He is currently working towards degrees in Neurology and Yoga Education. Michael practices an eclectic synthesis of Chiropractic and Thai Massage Therapy. And he likes to sing.

We study anatomy and physiology becuse spiritual perception is somatic, and the body is the vehicle for all sensation and perception, inner and outer.

—Michael Rosen-Pyros